Unleash Your Calm:

Navigating Life's Storms with Grace and Inner Peace

By

James C. Tanner

****

Unleash Your Calm:

Navigating Life's Storms with Grace and Inner Peace

****

Dedication

This book is dedicated to Maria, whose unending dedication to kindness, gratitude and positive lifestyle has touched so many lives.

****

****

****

Introduction

Welcome to "Unleash Your Calm: Navigating Life's Storms with Grace and Inner Peace". In this book, we will journey alongside four individuals, each with their unique struggles and triumphs. Their stories are being shared as they represent many of the same challenges we all face in our quest to walk through life filled with inner peace.

Beth is a dedicated nurse who thrives on helping others. However, the demands of her profession, combined with the emotional toll of patient care, have left her grappling with overwhelming stress and anxiety. She often finds herself lying awake at night, her mind racing with worries about her patients and the never-ending to-do list.

Sam is a successful entrepreneur who has built his business from the ground up. While he takes pride in his achievements, the constant pressure to innovate and stay ahead of the competition has led to a relentless inner critic. Sam struggles with negative self-talk, often doubting his decisions and fearing failure.

Chuck is a devoted father and a financial analyst. The recent economic downturn has put his job at risk, and he's struggling to maintain a sense of calm amidst the uncertainty. The stress of potentially losing his income while supporting his family has made it challenging for him to find peace and balance in his life.

Debbie is a creative writer who finds joy in storytelling. Yet, the solitude of her craft, combined with the pressures of deadlines and self-imposed expectations, has led to a struggle with balancing her passion and her well-being. She often feels torn between her desire to create and her need for harmony in her life.

Through the stories of Beth, Sam, Chuck, and Debbie, " Unleash Your Calm: Navigating Life's Storms with Grace and Inner Peace", will explore practical strategies for managing stress, overcoming negative thoughts, and finding balance amidst life's storms. Join us on this journey to discover how to navigate life's challenges with grace and inner peace.

In today's fast-paced world, many of us are quietly suffering our way through life, struggling to cope with overwhelming stress and anxiety from both personal and professional realms. The pressures of modern living have led to a widespread struggle with negative thoughts and toxic self-talk, making it challenging to maintain inner peace and calm in the face of turbulent times.

The Prevalence of Stress and Anxiety

Stress and anxiety are not just personal issues; they are global phenomena. According to the American Institute of Stress, about 33% of people report feeling extreme stress, with 77% experiencing stress that impacts their physical health and 73% having stress that affects their mental health. The World Health Organization has even dubbed stress the "health epidemic of the 21st century."

In the workplace, the situation is equally dire. The American Psychological Association's 2021 Work and Well-being Survey found that 79% of employees had experienced work-related stress in the month prior to the survey, with 36% reporting cognitive weariness and 32% feeling emotionally exhausted.

The Struggle with Negative Thoughts and Toxic Self-Talk

Negative thoughts and toxic self-talk are pervasive issues that compound the effects of stress and anxiety. These patterns of thinking can lead to a vicious cycle, where negative thoughts breed more stress, and more stress breeds further negative thoughts. A study published in the Journal of Personality and Social Psychology found that rumination, or the tendency to dwell on negative thoughts, is a significant predictor of psychological distress.

Challenges in Maintaining Inner Peace and Calm

Maintaining inner peace and calm in turbulent times is a challenge many of us face. The constant barrage of negative news, social media pressures, and the demands of daily life can make it difficult to find a sense of tranquility. A survey conducted by the American Psychological Association revealed that 87% of Americans felt that watching the news caused them stress, highlighting the impact of external factors on our inner peace.

Struggling to Find Balance and Harmony Amidst Chaos

Finding balance and harmony amidst chaos is a struggle that resonates with many. The demands of work, family, and personal obligations can pull us in different directions, making it difficult to achieve a sense of equilibrium. A study published in the Journal of Applied Psychology found that work-family conflict is a significant source of stress, with 60% of respondents reporting high levels of conflict between their work and family responsibilities.

The Need for Practical Ways to Cope with Life's Pressures

Given the challenges we face, there is a desperate need to discover practical ways to cope with life's pressures. Mindfulness meditation, exercise, and therapy are some of the coping mechanisms that have been shown to be effective in managing stress and anxiety. A meta-analysis published in JAMA Internal Medicine found that mindfulness meditation programs had moderate evidence of improved anxiety, depression, and pain.

The struggle to cope with overwhelming stress and anxiety, manage negative thoughts and toxic self-talk, maintain inner peace and calm, find balance and harmony, and discover practical ways to cope with life's pressures is a reality for many of us. It's important to recognize that these challenges are not insurmountable. By seeking support, adopting healthy coping mechanisms, and prioritizing self-care, we can navigate life's storms with grace and inner peace.

****

Chapter 1

Understanding Your Storm:

Recognizing Stress and Its Triggers

Sam, now in his late 20's, had come from a family of fairly successful entrepreneurs. His mother and father had built up a successful water and oil pump parts supply company in the heart of the mid-west. Sam's siblings' each had moved on to big city life, to build their own businesses. Family reunions saw the driveway fill with the newest model of cars and trucks. Family reunion dinner table discussions were centred on how each of their businesses were growing and doing well. Only Sam was silent, smiling and nodding his head as he listened earnestly.

Not as well educated as his siblings, Sam had opted to stay closer to home attending the local community college while helping his folks with emergency weekend calls for parts deliveries. The other siblings has gone to the larger cities to obtain university degrees in a wide range of business administration disciplines.

Since leaving college, Sam had taken his nest egg and tried to break out in the online world. At first, he was doing well, or so he thought. He had invested heavily into "up-to-date" training and software, failing to realize that in the online world, change happens fast, and a course can be outdated and cast into the pool of relics within 6 months. Now three years into his business, his nest egg was gone, he was in debt to an uncomfortable level, and behind two years on his taxes. Profits were a "someday" dream for Sam.

As the family gathered at the reunion table, Sam would quietly share how all was going well, and how excited he was about the future of his business. What he didn't share was his new daily struggle with high blood pressure, the stress night sweats that would soak his bedding each night. His fear of answering the phone in case it was a creditor or tax man calling. Sam didn't share how some days he would read the obituaries and feel jealous when an obituary of a friend would show up. Life stress was real for Sam – he was drowning in it.

Debbie's story is similar in some ways to Sam's. She is a creative writer who finds joy in storytelling. Her independent spirit and entrepreneurial heart is incredibly strong within her. Yet, the solitude of her craft, combined with the pressures of deadlines and self-imposed expectations, has led to a struggle with balancing her passion and her well-being. Her craft gives her great joy, but she is a true example of "a starving artist". She often feels torn between her desire to create and her need for stress free harmony in her life.

Stress, an omnipresent force, has become a defining feature of modern existence, affecting individuals across the globe. A staggering 75% of adults report experiencing moderate to high levels of stress this past month, with 1 in 75 people possibly experiencing panic disorder. These statistics highlight a universal struggle, underscoring that people like Sam are not alone in their experiences.

As we begin to delve into the subject matter of overwhelming stress, we want to begin by defining stress and distinguishing between its two forms: eustress, which can be beneficial and motivating, and distress, which can be harmful and debilitating. Understanding this distinction is crucial, as it shapes our approach to managing stress. We then explore the multifaceted ways stress influences our physical health, emotional well-being, and cognitive functioning. From tension headaches to anxiety, the manifestations of stress are diverse and far-reaching.

Identifying common triggers of stress is our next focus. In today's fast-paced world, sources of stress are abundant, ranging from work pressures and relationship issues to financial concerns and health problems. We examine the role of perceived control and unpredictability, highlighting how our reactions to stressors can either exacerbate or alleviate our stress levels.

The connection between stress and negative thinking is a critical aspect of our discussion. Stress often breeds a cycle of toxic self-talk and negative thoughts, such as catastrophizing and black-and-white thinking. Breaking this cycle is essential for regaining inner peace and maintaining mental clarity.

Recognizing the symptoms and warning signs of stress is vital for timely intervention. We provide a comprehensive list of indicators, including physical, emotional, and behavioral signs, to help you identify when stress is taking a toll on your well-being. Self-awareness is the first step toward effective stress management.

Finally, we address the challenge of achieving stress and life balance. In a world where chaos often reigns, finding harmony and balance is paramount. We introduce the concept of work-life balance and discuss its significance in managing stress effectively. By prioritizing our well-being and adopting practical strategies, we can navigate life's storms with grace and inner peace.

This chapter serves as a foundation for the subsequent steps in our 7-step process to regain inner peace. By understanding your storm and recognizing the triggers of stress, you are better equipped to embark on a journey toward a calmer, more balanced life.

Defining stress and its Impact on well-being is a crucial starting point for understanding how to navigate life's challenges with grace and inner peace. In this section, we'll explore the nature of stress, its different forms, and its wide-ranging effects on our physical and mental health.

What is Stress?

Stress is a natural response of the body and mind to demands or challenges. It's the body's way of preparing to meet a tough situation with focus, stamina, strength, and heightened alertness. The renowned endocrinologist Hans Selye, who first identified and documented stress, defined it as "the non-specific response of the body to any demand for change" (Selye, 1936).

Types of Stress: Eustress vs. Distress

Not all stress is bad. In fact, stress can be categorized into two types: eustress and distress.

- **Eustress**, or positive stress, is the type of stress that motivates and energizes us. It's associated with adrenaline rushes, such as those experienced during a thrilling roller coaster ride or when we're pushing ourselves to achieve a personal goal. Eustress is often short-term and feels within our coping abilities. It's what keeps us vital and excited about life.
- **Distress**, on the other hand, is negative stress. It's the type of stress that feels overwhelming and beyond our control. Distress can be acute (short-term) or chronic (long-term), and it can lead to physical and psychological problems if not managed properly.

Stress can have profound effects on our well-being, impacting our physical health, emotional state, and cognitive functioning.

When we're stressed, our body releases stress hormones like cortisol and adrenaline. While these hormones are useful in short bursts, prolonged exposure can lead to health issues such as high blood pressure, heart disease, obesity, diabetes, and a weakened immune system. Stress can also manifest physically in the form of headaches, muscle tension, fatigue, and sleep disturbances.

Chronic stress can lead to a range of emotional issues, including anxiety, depression, irritability, and mood swings. It can also diminish our sense of joy, peace, and fulfillment in life. When we're constantly in a state of stress, it's challenging to maintain a positive outlook and enjoy our daily experiences.

Stress can affect our cognitive abilities, leading to difficulties with concentration, memory, decision-making, and problem-solving. It can make us more prone to mental fatigue and reduce our overall productivity and effectiveness in both personal and professional settings.

Managing Stress for Better Well-being

Understanding the nature and impact of stress is the first step toward managing it effectively. By recognizing the signs of stress and identifying its sources in our lives, we can employ strategies to reduce its negative effects and enhance our overall well-being. Subsequent sections of this chapter will delve into identifying common stress triggers and exploring practical techniques for stress management.

Stress is an inherent part of life, but its impact on our well-being depends on how we respond to it. By differentiating between eustress and distress and being mindful of stress's effects on our physical, emotional, and cognitive health, we can take proactive steps to manage stress and cultivate a sense of inner peace and balance.

Identifying Common Triggers of Stress

Understanding the common triggers of stress is crucial in managing it effectively. Stress can stem from various sources, each affecting individuals differently based on their unique circumstances and perceptions. Let's explore some of these common stressors and the role of perceived control and unpredictability in contributing to stress levels.

The workplace is a significant source of stress for many people. Deadlines, workload, job insecurity, and interpersonal conflicts can all contribute to heightened stress levels. The pressure to perform and meet expectations can be overwhelming, leading to anxiety and burnout. For some, the stress might come from a lack of fulfillment or feeling undervalued in their job roles.

Interpersonal relationships, whether with a partner, family members, or friends, can also be a major source of stress. Communication breakdowns, trust issues, and conflicts can strain relationships, causing emotional distress. For some, the fear of loneliness or the pressure to maintain social connections can be stressful.

Money problems are a common stressor for many individuals. The stress of managing debt, saving for the future, or simply making ends meet can be a constant source of worry. Economic instability and financial uncertainty can exacerbate these concerns, leading to anxiety about one's financial security.

Personal health issues or caring for a loved one with health problems can be a significant source of stress. Chronic illnesses, medical treatments, and the uncertainty of health outcomes can lead to feelings of helplessness and anxiety. The impact of health on one's quality of life and future prospects can be a constant worry.

Perceived Control and Unpredictability

The role of perceived control and unpredictability is crucial in understanding how these stressors affect us. When we feel in control of a situation, we are more likely to view it as a challenge rather than a stressor. However, when situations feel unpredictable or beyond our control, they can contribute significantly to our stress levels. The uncertainty of not knowing what will happen or feeling unable to influence outcomes can be particularly distressing.

For instance, in the workplace, having autonomy and decision-making power can reduce stress, while micromanagement and lack of control can increase it. In relationships, feeling secure and having open communication can mitigate stress, while unpredictability in a partner's behavior can heighten it. Financial stability provides a sense of control, whereas unexpected expenses or job loss can lead to stress. In terms of health, having a clear treatment plan and support system can provide a sense of control, while an uncertain prognosis can be a significant stressor.

Identifying the sources of stress in our lives is the first step toward managing them effectively. By understanding the common triggers of stress and the role of perceived control and unpredictability, we can develop strategies to cope with stress more effectively. In the following sections, we will explore practical techniques for managing stress and regaining a sense of balance and well-being.

The Connection Between Stress and Negative Thinking

The connection between stress and negative thinking is a critical aspect of our mental well-being. Stress can often act as a catalyst for negative thoughts and toxic self-talk, creating a vicious cycle that can be challenging to break. Understanding this connection and the cognitive distortions that come with it is essential for managing stress and fostering a healthier mindset.

Stress can trigger a cascade of negative thoughts, which in turn can increase our stress levels. This cycle can be particularly damaging because it not only exacerbates our current stress but also impacts our ability to cope with future stressors. For example, when we're stressed about a work deadline, we might start thinking, "I'll never get this done on time," which increases our anxiety and makes it even harder to focus and be productive.

When we're under stress, our brain's fight-or-flight response is activated, and our thinking patterns can become more negative and irrational. We might engage in toxic self-talk, such as "I'm not good enough" or "I can't handle this," which further undermines our confidence and ability to cope. This negative self-talk can become a self-fulfilling prophecy, where we believe we're incapable of handling stress, and as a result, we actually become less capable.

Cognitive Distortions in Stressful Situations

Cognitive distortions are irrational or exaggerated thinking patterns that can contribute to negative emotions and behaviors. They are particularly common in stressful situations. Two common cognitive distortions are catastrophizing and black-and-white thinking:

- **Catastrophizing**: This is when we anticipate the worst possible outcome in a situation, even when it's unlikely. For example, if we make a small mistake at work, we might think, "I'm going to get fired," even though the mistake is fixable and unlikely to have such severe consequences.
- **Black-and-White Thinking**: Also known as all-or-nothing thinking, this distortion involves seeing things in extreme, either/or terms. For example, if we don't perform perfectly in a presentation, we might think, "I'm a complete failure," rather than recognizing that everyone makes mistakes and

that we can learn and improve from the experience.

Breaking the cycle of stress and negative thinking requires awareness and intentional effort.

Practicing mindfulness can help us become more aware of our thoughts and feelings without getting caught up in them. Meditation can provide a sense of calm and clarity, helping us break free from the cycle of negative thinking.

Techniques such as cognitive restructuring can help us challenge and change irrational thoughts, while behavioral activation can help us engage in activities that boost our mood and reduce stress.

Being kind to ourselves and acknowledging that everyone experiences stress and makes mistakes can help reduce the impact of negative self-talk.

Sometimes, talking to a friend, family member, or mental health professional can provide a different perspective and help us challenge our negative thoughts.

The connection between stress and negative thinking is a complex interplay that can significantly impact our mental health. By understanding this connection and employing strategies to manage it, we can reduce the impact of stress on our lives and foster a more positive and resilient mindset.

Recognizing Symptoms and Warning Signs

Recognizing the symptoms and warning signs of stress is crucial for managing it effectively. Stress can manifest in various physical, emotional, and behavioral ways, and being aware of these signs can help you take proactive steps to reduce its impact on your life.

Stress can have a significant impact on your physical health. Some common physical symptoms of stress include:

- **Headaches**: Stress can trigger tension headaches or migraines.
- **Muscle Tension**: You might experience tightness in your neck, shoulders, or back.
- **Fatigue**: Feeling unusually tired or experiencing a lack of energy is common.
- **Sleep Disturbances**: This can include trouble falling asleep, staying asleep, or experiencing restless sleep.
- **Digestive Issues**: Stress can lead to stomach aches, nausea, or changes in appetite.
- **Rapid Heartbeat**: You might notice your heart racing or palpitations.
- **Sweating**: Excessive sweating, particularly in the palms, is a physical sign of stress.

Stress can also affect your emotional well-being. Some emotional symptoms of stress include:

- **Anxiety**: Feeling nervous, restless, or constantly worried.
- **Irritability**: You might find yourself snapping at others or feeling easily agitated.
- **Depression**: Prolonged stress can lead to feelings of sadness or hopelessness.
- **Mood Swings**: Experiencing rapid changes in mood or feeling emotionally unstable.
- **Feeling Overwhelmed**: The sensation of being unable to cope with the demands of life.

Stress can influence your behavior in noticeable ways. Some behavioral symptoms of stress include:

- **Changes in Eating Habits**: This can include overeating or undereating.
- **Procrastination**: Putting off tasks or avoiding responsibilities.
- **Increased Use of Substances**: Turning to alcohol, drugs, or cigarettes as a coping mechanism.
- **Social Withdrawal**: Avoiding social interactions or activities you once enjoyed.
- **Nervous Behaviors**: Such as nail-biting, fidgeting, or pacing.

Encouraging Self-Awareness

Self-awareness is key to managing stress. It involves recognizing your stress triggers, understanding how stress affects you, and monitoring your stress levels. Here are some tips to enhance self-awareness:

- **Keep a Stress Journal**: Record your stress levels, triggers, and how you respond to stress. This can help you identify patterns and develop strategies to cope.
- **Practice Mindfulness**: Mindfulness techniques, such as meditation or deep breathing, can help you stay present and aware of your thoughts and feelings.
- **Listen to Your Body**: Pay attention to physical signs of stress and take proactive steps to relax and unwind.
- **Seek Feedback**: Sometimes, others might notice changes in your behavior before you do. Be open to feedback from friends or family about your stress levels.
- **Set Boundaries**: Knowing your limits and setting boundaries can help prevent stress from overwhelming you.

By recognizing the symptoms and warning signs of stress and cultivating self-awareness, you can take control of your stress levels and improve your overall well-being. Remember, it's essential to seek support from friends, family, or mental health professionals if you're struggling to manage stress on your own.

Stress and Life Balance

Maintaining balance and harmony in different areas of life, especially when under stress, is a challenge that many of us face. In this modern world, where the pace of life is faster than ever, finding equilibrium between work, personal life, and other responsibilities can seem like an elusive goal. This section explores the concept of work-life balance and its significance in managing stress effectively.

Life is a juggling act, with each of us trying to keep multiple balls in the air - work, family, health, social life, personal growth, and more. When stress enters the picture, it can throw off our balance, leading to a feeling of being overwhelmed and out of control. Stress can make it difficult to prioritize our responsibilities and can lead to neglect in certain areas of our lives.

For example, a demanding job might encroach on time meant for family or self-care, leading to strained relationships and personal dissatisfaction. On the other hand, personal issues can distract from professional responsibilities, impacting work performance and career progression.

Work-life balance is about finding a healthy equilibrium between professional and personal activities. It's not about dividing your time equally but about allocating it in a way that contributes to your overall well-being and fulfillment.

Achieving work-life balance is crucial for managing stress effectively. When we have balance, we're better equipped to handle the pressures of life without becoming overwhelmed. It allows us to be present and engaged in whatever we're doing, whether it's meeting a work deadline or spending quality time with family.

Strategies for Achieving Work-Life Balance:

1. **Set Priorities**: Identify what's most important to you in both your personal and professional life. Allocate your time and energy accordingly.
2. **Establish Boundaries**: Set clear boundaries between work and personal life. This might mean not checking work emails after a certain time or ensuring you have uninterrupted family time.
3. **Learn to Say No**: Recognize that you can't do everything. Be selective about the commitments you take on, and don't be afraid to say no when necessary.
4. **Take Breaks**: Regular breaks are essential for maintaining balance. They help prevent burnout and keep you refreshed and focused.
5. **Practice Self-Care**: Make time for activities that nurture your physical, emotional, and mental well-being. This could be exercise, meditation, hobbies, or simply relaxing.
6. **Seek Flexibility**: If possible, seek work arrangements that offer flexibility, such as flexible hours or the option to work remotely. This can help you better manage your time and reduce stress.
7. **Delegate**: You don't have to do everything yourself. Delegate tasks at work and home to share the load and free up time for other activities.
8. **Stay Organized**: Use tools like calendars, planners, and to-do lists to keep track of your responsibilities and commitments. This can help you manage your time more effectively.
9. **Communicate**: Keep open lines of communication with

> your employer, colleagues, and family about your needs and boundaries. This can help manage expectations and reduce conflicts.

10. **Reflect and Adjust**: Regularly assess your work-life balance and make adjustments as needed. Life is constantly changing, and what works at one time may not work at another.

Achieving work-life balance is a dynamic and ongoing process. It requires self-awareness, setting priorities, establishing boundaries, and being proactive in managing your time and responsibilities. By striving for balance, you can reduce stress, enhance your well-being, and lead a more fulfilling life.

Sam, without realizing it, had become the "Poster Boy" for those who struggle with stress. He is not alone. Many of us face this same challenge, but respond outwardly the same way Sam did at his family reunion dinner table when he'd say, "This are going great!"

Stress, as Sam was beginning to recognize, doesn't come along on it's own, and it sure doesn't leave on it's own either. It has to be managed, conquered, and put to rest.

As we draw to the end of this chapter titled "Understanding Your Storm: Recognizing Stress and Its Triggers," we have embarked on a journey to help us all unravel the complexities of stress and its profound impact on our lives. We delved into the essence of stress, distinguishing between the motivating force of eustress and the debilitating effects of distress. Through this exploration, we gained insight into how stress can manifest physically, emotionally, and behaviorally, affecting our overall well-being.

We identified common triggers of stress, such as work pressures, relationship issues, financial concerns, and health problems. By understanding these triggers, we can begin to recognize the situations and circumstances that elevate our stress levels. Furthermore, we explored the role of perceived control and unpredictability in exacerbating stress, highlighting the importance of feeling in command of our lives to mitigate stress's impact.

A significant focus of this chapter was on the intricate connection between stress and negative thinking. We examined how stress can fuel a cycle of toxic self-talk and negative thoughts, leading to cognitive distortions like catastrophizing and black-and-white thinking. Breaking free from this cycle is essential for regaining a sense of peace and clarity.

Recognizing the symptoms and warning signs of stress is crucial for timely intervention. We provided a comprehensive list of indicators to help you identify when stress is taking a toll on your well-being. By being aware of these signs, you can take proactive steps to address stress before it becomes overwhelming.

Finally, we discussed the challenge of maintaining balance and harmony in different areas of life when under stress. The concept of work-life balance was introduced as a key strategy for managing stress effectively. By striving for equilibrium between our professional and personal lives, we can reduce stress and enhance our overall quality of life.

As we conclude this chapter, we lay the groundwork for the next step in our journey: "Calming the Seas: The Power of Mindfulness and Meditation." In the upcoming chapter, we will explore how mindfulness and meditation can be transformative tools in navigating the tumultuous waters of stress. These practices offer a pathway to inner peace, helping us to cultivate a sense of calm and presence in the midst of life's storms. By embracing mindfulness and meditation, we can learn to ride the waves of stress with grace and emerge with a deeper sense of serenity and balance.

****

Chapter 2

Calming the Seas:

The Power of Mindfulness and Meditation

In this chapter titled "Calming the Seas: The Power of Mindfulness and Meditation," we delve into the transformative power of mindfulness and meditation as foundational techniques for achieving inner peace and reducing stress. Amidst the turbulent waves of life, these practices offer a sanctuary of calm, enabling us to navigate our personal and professional challenges with grace and balance.

Understanding Mindfulness and Meditation

Mindfulness and meditation are often used interchangeably, yet they hold distinct meanings. Mindfulness is the practice of being fully present and engaged in the moment, aware of our thoughts, feelings, bodily sensations, and surrounding environment without judgment. It's about observing our experiences as they unfold, allowing us to respond rather than react to life's stressors.

Meditation, on the other hand, is a formal practice that involves focusing the mind on a particular object, thought, or activity to train attention and awareness. It's a deliberate practice that cultivates mindfulness and fosters a deep sense of inner peace.

A wealth of research supports the effectiveness of mindfulness and meditation in reducing stress and anxiety and improving overall well-being. Studies have shown that these practices can lead to changes in brain structure, such as increased gray matter density in areas associated with memory, empathy, and stress regulation.

Physiologically, mindfulness and meditation can lower blood pressure, reduce chronic pain, and improve sleep quality.

Incorporating mindfulness into daily life doesn't require special equipment or extensive training. Simple techniques such as mindful breathing, where we focus our attention on our breath, can provide an anchor to the present moment. The body scan is another technique that involves paying attention to each part of the body in turn, noticing any sensations or tension. Mindful eating and walking meditation are practices that transform everyday activities into opportunities for mindfulness.

Starting a meditation practice can be as simple as setting aside a few minutes each day to sit quietly and focus on the breath. There are various types of meditation, including concentration meditation, where the focus is on a single point, and loving-kindness meditation, which involves cultivating feelings of compassion and kindness. Visualization techniques can also be powerful tools in meditation, helping to create a sense of inner calm and clarity.

Making mindfulness and meditation a part of our everyday routines can significantly enhance our ability to manage stress and maintain a sense of balance. Creating a dedicated meditation space, using mindfulness in stressful situations, and finding community support through meditation groups or online forums can help sustain a regular practice.

A Deeper Understanding of Mindfulness and Meditation

In the modern world, where stress and anxiety often dominate our lives, finding ways to achieve inner peace and reduce stress is essential. Mindfulness and meditation are two practices that have gained popularity for their ability to bring about a sense of calm and balance. While they are often used interchangeably, mindfulness and meditation are distinct practices, each with its own benefits and principles.

Mindfulness is the practice of being fully present and engaged in the moment, without judgment. It involves paying attention to our thoughts, feelings, bodily sensations, and the environment around us with an attitude of curiosity and acceptance. Mindfulness can be practiced at any moment, whether we are eating, walking, or simply breathing.

Meditation, on the other hand, is a more formal practice that involves setting aside time to focus the mind and achieve a state of deep relaxation and concentration. There are various forms of meditation, but most involve techniques such as focusing on the breath, repeating a mantra, or visualizing a peaceful scene.

Mindfulness has its roots in ancient Buddhist traditions, where it was practiced as a way to cultivate awareness and insight. In the 1970s, Dr. Jon Kabat-Zinn, a molecular biologist, adapted mindfulness principles to create the Mindfulness-Based Stress Reduction (MBSR) program, which brought mindfulness into the mainstream of Western medicine and psychology.

Meditation also has a long history, with origins in religious and spiritual traditions around the world, including Buddhism, Hinduism, and Christianity. In recent years, meditation has been studied extensively for its health benefits, leading to a growing acceptance of the practice in the scientific and medical communities.

How Mindfulness and Meditation Contribute to Stress Reduction and Inner Peace

Mindfulness and meditation offer powerful tools for managing stress and finding inner peace. By bringing our attention to the present moment, mindfulness helps us break free from the cycle of rumination and worry that often accompanies stress. It allows us to observe our thoughts and emotions without getting caught up in them, leading to a greater sense of calm and clarity.

Meditation, through its focus on relaxation and concentration, can activate the body's relaxation response, a physiological state that counteracts the stress response. Regular meditation practice has been shown to reduce levels of the stress hormone cortisol, lower blood pressure, and improve sleep quality.

The benefits of mindfulness and meditation extend beyond stress reduction. Research has shown that these practices can improve mental health, enhance cognitive function, and boost emotional well-being. Mindfulness has been used effectively as a therapeutic tool for treating anxiety, depression, and chronic pain. Meditation has been linked to increased gray matter density in areas of the brain associated with memory, empathy, and self-awareness.

Incorporating mindfulness and meditation into daily life doesn't require significant time or effort. Simple practices such as taking a few minutes each day to focus on the breath, practicing mindful eating, or engaging in a short meditation session can make a profound difference in our overall well-being. The key is to approach these practices with patience and consistency, allowing their benefits to unfold over time.

Mindfulness and meditation offer accessible and effective ways to navigate the challenges of modern life with greater ease and tranquility. By understanding and embracing these practices, we can cultivate a sense of inner peace, reduce stress, and enhance our overall quality of life.

In recent years, the scientific community has shown a growing interest in understanding the effects of mindfulness and meditation on the human mind and body. A wealth of research now supports the effectiveness of these practices in reducing stress, anxiety, and improving overall well-being. This section explores some of the key findings from studies on brain changes, physiological benefits, and mental health improvements associated with mindfulness and meditation.

One of the most fascinating areas of research is the impact of mindfulness and meditation on the brain. Neuroimaging studies have shown that regular meditation can lead to structural changes in the brain, often referred to as neuroplasticity.

Studies have found that meditation is associated with increased gray matter density in areas of the brain involved in memory, empathy, and self-awareness, such as the hippocampus and prefrontal cortex (Hölzel et al., 2011).

Mindfulness meditation has been shown to enhance connectivity between different regions of the brain, leading to improved emotional regulation and cognitive function (Kilpatrick et al., 2011).

The amygdala, known as the brain's "fear center," shows reduced activity in individuals who practice meditation regularly, indicating a decrease in stress and anxiety responses (Desbordes et al., 2012).

The practice of mindfulness and meditation also brings about significant physiological benefits, helping to improve overall physical health.

Meditation has been found to lower blood pressure, reducing the risk of heart disease and stroke (Anderson et al., 2008).

Mindfulness meditation has been linked to enhanced immune function, with studies showing increased antibody production following mindfulness training (Davidson et al., 2003).

Research suggests that mindfulness meditation can reduce inflammation markers in the body, which are associated with a variety of chronic diseases (Rosenkranz et al., 2013).

One of the most compelling reasons for the popularity of mindfulness and meditation is their ability to improve mental health.

Numerous studies have shown that mindfulness-based interventions can significantly reduce symptoms of anxiety and depression (Hofmann et al., 2010).

Mindfulness and meditation practices have been shown to enhance resilience, enabling individuals to cope more effectively with stress (Creswell et al., 2016).

By fostering greater awareness of thoughts and emotions, mindfulness meditation can improve emotional regulation, leading to more balanced and positive emotional states (Teper et al., 2013).

The science of mindfulness and meditation provides compelling evidence of their benefits for both the mind and body. By promoting changes in the brain, improving physiological health, and enhancing mental well-being, these practices offer a powerful tool for reducing stress and anxiety and improving overall quality of life. As research continues to unfold, it is clear that mindfulness and meditation hold great promise for fostering a healthier, more balanced, and more peaceful life.

Practical Techniques for Mindfulness

Incorporating mindfulness into our daily lives can transform our experience of the world, bringing a sense of calm and clarity amid the hustle and bustle of modern living. Mindfulness is not just a practice but a way of being, a lens through which we can observe life more attentively and compassionately. This section will introduce various practical mindfulness techniques, including mindful breathing, body scan, mindful eating, and walking meditation, providing step-by-step guidance for incorporating these practices into your daily routine.

Mindful breathing is a foundational mindfulness practice that focuses on the breath as an anchor to the present moment. Here's how you can practice mindful breathing:

1. **Find a Quiet Place**: Sit or lie down in a comfortable position in a quiet space where you won't be disturbed.
2. **Focus on Your Breath**: Close your eyes and bring your attention to your breath. Notice the sensation of the air flowing in and out of your nostrils or the rise and fall of your chest and abdomen.
3. **Observe Without Judgment**: When your mind wanders, gently acknowledge the thoughts and return your focus to your breath. The goal is not to stop thinking but to observe your thoughts without judgment.
4. **Practice Regularly**: Start with a few minutes each day and gradually increase the duration. Consistency is key to developing mindfulness.

The body scan is a mindfulness practice that involves paying attention to different parts of the body in a systematic way.

Lie down on your back with your arms at your sides, palms facing up. Close your eyes and take a few deep breaths to relax.

Starting from the top of your head, bring your attention to each part of your body in turn. Notice any sensations, tension, or discomfort without trying to change anything.

Slowly move your attention down your body, from your head to your neck, shoulders, arms, chest, abdomen, back, hips, legs, and feet.

Once you've scanned your entire body, take a few deep breaths and slowly open your eyes. Reflect on the experience and notice any changes in your body or mind.

Mindful eating is the practice of bringing full attention to the experience of eating, savoring each bite, and listening to your body's hunger and fullness cues. Begin with a small amount of food on your plate to avoid mindless overeating. Before you start eating, take a moment to appreciate the colors, smells, and textures of your food. Take small bites and chew your food thoroughly. Put down your utensils between bites to slow down the pace. Notice how your body feels as you eat. Are you still hungry, or are you starting to feel full? Mindful eating is about listening to your body's signals, not just eating until the plate is empty. After the meal, take a moment to reflect on your experience. How do you feel physically and emotionally? What did you notice about the food and your eating habits?

Walking meditation is a form of mindfulness practice that involves walking slowly and deliberately, paying attention to each step:

1. **Choose a Quiet Path**: Find a quiet place where you can walk back and forth or in a circle without distractions.
2. **Start with Intention**: Stand still for a moment and set an intention for your walking meditation. Take a few deep breaths to center yourself.
3. **Focus on Your Feet**: As you start walking, focus your attention on the sensation of your feet touching the ground. Notice the movement of your legs and the rhythm of your steps.
4. **Walk Slowly**: Walk at a slower pace than usual, allowing yourself to be fully present with each step. If your mind

wanders, gently bring your attention back to your feet and the act of walking.

5. **Practice Mindful Awareness**: Expand your awareness to include the sights, sounds, and smells around you. Notice how your body feels as you move through space.

Incorporating these practical mindfulness techniques into your daily life can help you cultivate a sense of inner peace and well-being. Whether it's taking a few minutes to breathe mindfully, doing a body scan before bed, eating with full awareness, or turning your daily walk into a meditation, mindfulness offers a pathway to a more present and fulfilling life.

Meditation for Beginners

Embarking on a journey into meditation can be a transformative experience that brings a sense of peace, clarity, and well-being to your life. As a beginner, navigating the world of meditation may seem daunting, but with some guidance and understanding, you can establish a practice that suits your individual needs and preferences. This section provides a beginner's guide to meditation, exploring different types of meditation, tips for setting up a regular practice, and addressing common challenges and misconceptions.

Meditation is a practice that involves training your mind to focus and redirect your thoughts. It has been used for centuries in various cultures and traditions to cultivate mindfulness, reduce stress, and enhance personal and spiritual growth. At its core, meditation is about being present in the moment and observing your thoughts and feelings without judgment.

There are many types of meditation, each with its own focus and techniques. Here are a few popular ones that are suitable for beginners:

1. **Concentration Meditation**: This type of meditation involves focusing your attention on a single point, such as your breath, a mantra, or a candle flame. The goal is to cultivate a deep sense of focus and calm by continuously bringing your mind back to the object of concentration whenever it wanders.

2. **Loving-Kindness Meditation (Metta)**: Loving-kindness meditation is about cultivating feelings of compassion and kindness toward yourself and others. It involves silently repeating phrases of goodwill and positive wishes, such as "May I be happy, may I be healthy, may I be safe."

3. **Visualization Meditation**: In this form of meditation, you focus on a mental image or scene that evokes a sense of peace and relaxation. Visualization can be a powerful tool for reducing stress and promoting emotional well-being.

4. **Mindfulness Meditation**: Mindfulness meditation is about being fully present and aware of your experiences without judgment. It involves observing your thoughts, feelings, and sensations as they arise and pass, helping you develop a deeper understanding of your mind and body.

Establishing a regular meditation practice is key to reaping the benefits of meditation. Here are some tips to help you get started:

- **Find a Quiet Space**: Choose a quiet and comfortable place where you can meditate without interruptions.

- **Set a Schedule**: Try to meditate at the same time each day to establish a routine. Even just a few minutes daily can make a difference.

- **Start Small**: Begin with short sessions, such as 5-10 minutes, and gradually increase the duration as you become more comfortable.

- **Use Guided Meditations**: As a beginner, guided meditations can be helpful in providing structure and guidance. There are many apps and online resources available that offer guided meditations for various purposes.

- **Be Patient and Consistent**: Meditation is a skill that takes time to develop. Be patient with yourself and commit to practicing regularly.

Common Challenges and Misconceptions

A common misconception is that meditation is about stopping your thoughts. In reality, it's about observing your thoughts without getting caught up in them. It's natural for your mind to wander; the practice is in gently bringing it back to your focus.

Many beginners find it challenging to concentrate during meditation. This is normal. With time and practice, your ability to focus will improve.

Restlessness and boredom can arise during meditation. Acknowledge these feelings without judgment and gently redirect your attention to your chosen focus.

Meditation is a gradual process. It's important to approach it with an open mind and without expectations for immediate results.

Meditation is a journey of self-discovery and personal growth. By understanding the different types of meditation, setting up a regular practice, and navigating common challenges, you can embark on a path toward greater mindfulness, peace, and well-being. Remember, the most important part of meditation is showing up for yourself with kindness and patience.

Integrating Mindfulness and Meditation into Daily Life

Incorporating mindfulness and meditation into daily life can transform the way we experience the world, helping us navigate stress and maintain a sense of calm and balance. While it may seem challenging to fit these practices into a busy schedule, there are numerous ways to seamlessly integrate mindfulness and meditation into everyday routines.

Mindfulness can be a powerful tool in managing stress and anxiety. Here are some strategies for using mindfulness in stressful situations:

- **Pause and Breathe**: When you feel overwhelmed, take a moment to pause and focus on your breath. Deep, slow breaths can help calm the mind and body.
- **Observe Your Thoughts**: Instead of getting caught up in your thoughts, try to observe them as if you're an outsider. This can help you detach from the stress and gain perspective.
- **Stay Present**: Bring your attention to the present moment. Focus on your surroundings, the sensations in your body, or the task at hand. This can help you break free from the cycle of worry and rumination.

Having a dedicated space for meditation can enhance your practice and make it easier to integrate into your daily life. Here are some tips for creating a meditation space:

- **Choose a Quiet Spot**: Find a quiet corner in your home where you can meditate without distractions. It doesn't have to be a large space, just a peaceful spot where you can sit comfortably.

- **Make It Comfortable**: Add cushions, a chair, or a meditation bench to make your space comfortable for sitting. You might also want to include a blanket or shawl to keep warm.
- **Personalize Your Space**: Decorate your meditation space with items that inspire a sense of calm and serenity, such as candles, incense, plants, or soothing artwork.
- **Keep It Clutter-Free**: A clutter-free environment can help reduce mental clutter and promote a sense of tranquility.

Joining a mindfulness or meditation community can provide support, motivation, and a sense of connection. Here are some ways to find community support:

- **Local Meditation Groups**: Look for meditation groups or mindfulness classes in your area. Many yoga studios, community centers, and wellness centers offer group meditation sessions.
- **Online Communities**: There are numerous online communities and forums dedicated to mindfulness and meditation. Platforms like Insight Timer, Headspace, and Calm offer guided meditations and a community of like-minded individuals.
- **Mindfulness Apps**: Many mindfulness apps offer features that allow you to connect with others, share your progress, and participate in group challenges.
- **Retreats and Workshops**: Attending a mindfulness retreat or workshop can deepen your practice and connect you with others on a similar journey.

Mindfulness can be practiced in everyday activities, turning ordinary moments into opportunities for presence and awareness. Here are some ways to incorporate mindfulness into daily life:

- **Mindful Eating**: Pay attention to the flavors, textures, and sensations of your food. Eat slowly and savor each bite.
- **Mindful Walking**: Focus on the sensation of your feet touching the ground as you walk. Notice the sights, sounds, and smells around you.
- **Mindful Communication**: Listen attentively when speaking with others. Be present in your conversations and respond with intention.
- **Mindful Breaks**: Take short breaks throughout the day to practice deep breathing, stretch, or simply observe your surroundings.

Integrating mindfulness and meditation into daily life is a journey that requires patience and practice. By using mindfulness in stressful situations, creating a dedicated meditation space, finding community support, and incorporating mindfulness into everyday activities, you can cultivate a sense of inner peace and balance that permeates all aspects of your life.

References

- Anderson, J. W., Liu, C., & Kryscio, R. J. (2008). Blood pressure response to transcendental meditation: a meta-analysis. *American Journal of Hypertension*, 21(3), 310-316.
- Creswell, J. D., Pacilio, L. E., Lindsay, E. K., & Brown, K. W. (2016). Brief mindfulness meditation training alters psychological and neuroendocrine responses to social

evaluative stress. *Psychoneuroendocrinology*, 69, 48-58.

- Davidson, R. J., Kabat-Zinn, J., Schumacher, J., Rosenkranz, M., Muller, D., Santorelli, S. F., ... & Sheridan, J. F. (2003). Alterations in brain and immune function produced by mindfulness meditation. *Psychosomatic Medicine*, 65(4), 564-570.

- Desbordes, G., Negi, L. T., Pace, T. W., Wallace, B. A., Raison, C. L., & Schwartz, E. L. (2012). Effects of mindful-attention and compassion meditation training on amygdala response to emotional stimuli in an ordinary, non-meditative state. *Frontiers in Human Neuroscience*, 6(6), 292. Link

- Hofmann, S. G., Sawyer, A. T., Witt, A. A., & Oh, D. (2010). The effect of mindfulness-based therapy on anxiety and depression: A meta-analytic review. *Journal of Consulting and Clinical Psychology*, 78(2), 169-183.

- Hölzel, B. K., Carmody, J., Vangel, M., Congleton, C., Yerramsetti, S. M., Gard, T., & Lazar, S. W. (2011). Mindfulness practice leads to increases in regional brain gray matter density. *Psychiatry Research: Neuroimaging*, 191(1), 36-43.

- Kilpatrick, L. A., Suyenobu, B. Y., Smith, S. R., Bueller, J. A., Goodman, T., Creswell, J. D., ... & Naliboff, B. D. (2011). Impact of mindfulness-based stress reduction training on intrinsic brain connectivity. *NeuroImage*, 56(1), 290-298.

- Rosenkranz, M. A., Davidson, R. J., MacCoon, D. G., Sheridan, J. F., Kalin, N. H., & Lutz, A. (2013). A comparison of mindfulness-based stress reduction and an active control in modulation of neurogenic inflammation. *Brain, Behavior, and Immunity*, 27(1), 174-184.

- Teper, R., Segal, Z. V., & Inzlicht, M. (2013). Inside the mindful mind: How mindfulness enhances emotion regulation through improvements in executive control. *Current Directions in Psychological Science*, 22(6), 449-454.

****

Chapter 3

Navigating Negative Thoughts:

Strategies for Positive Transformation

Beth, now 46 years of age, has devoted her whole career to nursing. Beth is one of those angels who thrives on helping others. However, she works constantly in a world of sick and dying people–people who complain for legitimate reasons. The demands of her profession, combined with the emotional toll of patient care, have left her grappling with overwhelming stress and anxiety. Now Beth often finds herself lying awake at night, her mind racing with worries about her patients and whether or not she can be enough for them.

With three kids at home, and being a single mom who works long varying shifts, Beth not only had her hands full at work, but at home as well. In fact, Beth's kids had become so used to Beth not being there for them, that communication had broken down, and the kids were left to raise themselves. In one hand, Beth wondered if she could be enough for her patients at the hospital, while in the other hand, Beth knew she wasn't being enough for those at home whom she dearly loved. Beth's inner world had become a world of constant self-criticism, and inner feelings of being a failure.

It's an undeniable truth that we all face challenges in our personal and professional lives that can lead to overwhelming stress and anxiety. However, it's how we navigate these turbulent waters that determine our ability to maintain peace, balance, and harmony.

Our thoughts are powerful. They shape our perceptions, influence our emotions, and guide our actions. Negative thoughts and toxic self-talk can create a lens through which we view the world, often leading to increased stress and anxiety. This section delves into the concept of cognitive distortions – those pesky, irrational thought patterns that convince us of things that aren't true, like assuming the worst or overgeneralizing. By recognizing these distortions, we can begin to challenge them and reduce their grip on our mental and emotional well-being.

In the midst of life's challenges, it's easy to focus on what's going wrong. But what if we shifted our focus to what's going right? This is where the power of gratitude comes in. Gratitude isn't just about saying "thank you"; it's about recognizing the abundance in our lives, even in small doses. This section explores how expressing gratitude can rewire our brains to focus on positivity, reducing stress and fostering a more optimistic outlook on life.

Words have power – the power to hurt and the power to heal. Positive affirmations are intentional, empowering statements that can counteract negative thoughts and reprogram our mindset. This part of the chapter provides guidance on creating and using affirmations that resonate with you, turning them into a daily practice that uplifts and inspires.

Changing the way we think isn't an overnight process; it's a journey of self-discovery and practice. This section offers practical techniques for transforming negative thinking patterns into positive ones. From cognitive restructuring to reframing and mindfulness, we'll explore strategies that can help you observe your thoughts without judgment and choose a more positive perspective.

Finally, maintaining a positive mindset amidst life's ups and downs requires ongoing effort and self-care. This part of the chapter emphasizes the importance of setting boundaries, seeking support, and engaging in activities that nourish your mind, body, and spirit. By cultivating a balanced and positive mindset, you can navigate the challenges of life with greater ease and resilience.

As we journey through this chapter, remember that navigating negative thoughts is a skill that can be developed over time. With patience, practice, and compassion for yourself, you can transform your mindset and embrace a more positive, balanced way of living.

Understanding the Impact of Negative Thinking

Negative thinking and toxic self-talk are phenomena that many of us encounter in our daily lives. They are the inner voices that criticize, doubt, and belittle us, often leading to increased stress and anxiety. This section delves into the impact of negative thinking on our mental and emotional well-being and explores the concept of cognitive distortions that contribute to a negative mindset.

Negative thinking can have a profound impact on our overall well-being. It can:

- **Increase Stress and Anxiety**: Constantly focusing on the negative aspects of situations can lead to heightened stress levels and anxiety, as it keeps our minds in a state of worry and apprehension.
- **Lead to Depression**: Prolonged negative thinking can contribute to feelings of hopelessness and sadness, which are key symptoms of depression.
- **Affect Physical Health**: The mind-body connection is strong, and negative thinking can manifest physically, causing headaches, fatigue, and even chronic conditions like heart disease.
- **Impair Decision-Making**: When we're caught in a cycle of

negative thinking, it can cloud our judgment and make it difficult to make rational decisions.

- **Damage Relationships**: Negativity can push people away and strain relationships, as it can be challenging for others to be around someone who is constantly negative.

Cognitive distortions are irrational thought patterns that distort reality, often leading to negative thinking. Understanding these distortions is crucial in addressing negative thoughts. Some common cognitive distortions include:

- **All-or-Nothing Thinking**: Viewing situations in extreme, black-and-white terms, without recognizing the shades of gray. For example, thinking "I'm a complete failure" after making a small mistake.
- **Overgeneralization**: Drawing broad conclusions from a single event. For example, thinking "I'll never be good at this" after one unsuccessful attempt.
- **Catastrophizing**: Expecting the worst possible outcome in a situation. For example, thinking "This will ruin everything" over a minor issue.
- **Mind Reading**: Assuming you know what others are thinking without evidence. For example, thinking "They must think I'm incompetent" without any indication from others.
- **Should Statements**: Using "should," "must," or "ought to" statements can lead to feelings of guilt or inadequacy. For example, thinking "I should always be perfect."

Breaking free from negative thinking requires awareness and effort. Here are some strategies to help transform negative thoughts:

- **Identify Negative Thoughts**: The first step is to become aware of your negative thoughts and recognize them as cognitive distortions.
- **Challenge Negative Thoughts**: Once you've identified a negative thought, challenge its validity. Ask yourself if there's evidence to support it and if there are alternative explanations.
- **Reframe Negative Thoughts**: Try to reframe negative thoughts in a more positive or neutral light. For example, instead of thinking "I'm a failure," consider "I didn't succeed this time, but I can learn from this experience."
- **Practice Mindfulness**: Mindfulness can help you stay present and observe your thoughts without getting caught up in them.
- **Seek Support**: Talking to a therapist or counselor can provide guidance and support in addressing negative thinking patterns.

Understanding the impact of negative thinking and the role of cognitive distortions is crucial in promoting mental and emotional well-being. By becoming aware of these patterns and actively challenging and reframing negative thoughts, we can cultivate a more positive and balanced mindset.

The Power of Gratitude

In the hustle and bustle of daily life, it's easy to get caught up in what we don't have, what we wish were different, or what we think we're missing. We often focus on the negatives, the gaps, and the voids in our lives, forgetting to appreciate the abundance that surrounds us. This is where the power of gratitude comes into play. Gratitude is more than just saying "thank you." It's a profound practice that can transform our perspective, reduce stress, and foster a more positive outlook on life.

Gratitude is an acknowledgment of the goodness in our lives. It's about recognizing the value of what we have and the contributions of others to our well-being. When we express gratitude, we shift our focus from what's lacking to what's abundant. This simple act can have a profound impact on our mental and emotional state.

The practice of gratitude has been linked to a multitude of benefits. It can:

- **Reduce Stress and Anxiety**: By focusing on the positive aspects of our lives, we can reduce feelings of stress and anxiety. Gratitude helps us put our challenges into perspective and approach them with a calmer, more balanced mindset.
- **Improve Mood and Well-being**: Regularly expressing gratitude can enhance our mood and overall sense of well-being. It fosters a sense of joy and contentment, even in difficult times.
- **Enhance Relationships**: Gratitude can strengthen our relationships with others. When we express appreciation for the people in our lives, it deepens our connections and fosters mutual respect and kindness.
- **Boost Resilience**: Gratitude can help us build resilience, enabling us to bounce back from setbacks and challenges with greater ease. It provides a solid foundation of positivity that can sustain us through tough times.

It's easy to feel grateful when things are going well, but what about when times are tough? How do we cultivate gratitude when we don't feel particularly grateful? The key is to start small and be consistent.

- **Find the Silver Linings**: Even in difficult situations, there are often hidden blessings. Look for the small positives, the lessons learned, or the growth experienced.
- **Keep a Gratitude Journal**: Writing down a few things you're grateful for each day can help shift your focus and make gratitude a regular part of your life.
- **Express Gratitude to Others**: Take the time to thank the people in your life. A simple thank-you note, a kind word, or a small gesture can go a long way.
- **Practice Mindfulness**: Being present in the moment allows you to appreciate the small joys and pleasures that you might otherwise overlook.

Gratitude has a ripple effect. When we express gratitude, it not only uplifts our own spirits but also those of the people around us. It creates a positive cycle of appreciation and kindness that can spread far and wide.

The power of gratitude lies in its ability to transform our perspective, reduce stress, and foster a more positive outlook on life. By practicing gratitude regularly, even when we don't feel particularly grateful, we can cultivate a sense of abundance and joy that permeates all aspects of our lives.

Exploring Positive Affirmations

In the realm of personal growth and mental well-being, positive affirmations have emerged as a powerful tool to counteract negative thoughts and reprogram our mindset. These affirmations are simple yet profound statements that can help us cultivate a more optimistic outlook and embrace our inner potential.

Positive affirmations are positive phrases or statements used to challenge negative or unhelpful thoughts. They are designed to encourage a positive mindset and self-empowerment. When repeated regularly, affirmations can help reinforce positive beliefs and attitudes, contributing to a more positive outlook on life.

The power of positive affirmations lies in their ability to shift our focus from negative to positive thoughts. By affirming our strengths, capabilities, and worth, we can create a mental environment that nurtures growth and positivity. Positive affirmations can help:

- **Boost self-esteem**: Affirmations remind us of our value and worth, helping to increase our confidence.
- **Reduce negative self-talk**: By replacing negative thoughts with positive ones, we can break the cycle of self-criticism.
- **Enhance resilience**: Positive affirmations can provide motivation and encouragement, helping us to persevere through challenges.
- **Improve mood**: Focusing on positive statements can lift our spirits and reduce feelings of stress and anxiety.

For affirmations to be effective, they should be personalized and resonate with the individual. Here are some tips for creating affirmations that truly speak to you:

- **Be specific**: Tailor your affirmations to your personal goals, values, and aspirations.
- **Use present tense**: Frame your affirmations as if they are already true, e.g., "I am confident and capable," rather than "I will be confident and capable."
- **Keep them positive**: Focus on what you want to achieve or feel, rather than what you want to avoid.

- **Make them believable**: Choose affirmations that feel attainable and realistic to you, even if they are aspirational.

Examples of Positive Affirmations

Here are some examples of positive affirmations that can be adapted to suit your individual needs:

- "I am worthy of love and respect."
- "I believe in my ability to overcome challenges."
- "I am grateful for the abundance in my life."
- "I choose to focus on the positive aspects of every situation."
- "I am capable of achieving my goals and dreams."

To maximize the impact of positive affirmations, consider incorporating them into your daily routine:

- **Morning affirmations**: Start your day with a few minutes of affirmations to set a positive tone for the day.
- **Affirmation reminders**: Place affirmation cards or notes in visible places, such as on your bathroom mirror or computer monitor.
- **Meditation and affirmations**: Combine affirmations with meditation or mindfulness practices to deepen their impact.
- **Journaling**: Write down your affirmations in a journal, along with reflections on how they make you feel.

Positive affirmations are a simple yet powerful tool for fostering a positive mindset and enhancing our overall well-being. By exploring and embracing affirmations that resonate with us, we can cultivate a more optimistic outlook and empower ourselves to face life's challenges with confidence and grace.

Transforming Negative Thoughts into Positive Ones

In the journey of life, we often encounter obstacles that challenge our mental and emotional well-being. Negative thoughts can cloud our minds, casting shadows on our happiness and peace. However, with the right tools and techniques, we can transform these negative thoughts into positive ones, paving the way for a brighter, more optimistic outlook.

Our thoughts hold immense power over our lives. They influence our emotions, actions, and ultimately, our reality. Negative thoughts can lead to a cycle of negativity, affecting our mental health and overall quality of life. Recognizing the impact of our thoughts is the first step toward transformation.

Cognitive restructuring is a technique used in cognitive-behavioral therapy (CBT) to challenge and change negative thought patterns. It involves identifying irrational or unhelpful thoughts, examining the evidence for and against these thoughts, and then replacing them with more balanced, realistic ones. By questioning the validity of our negative thoughts, we can rewrite the narrative in our minds, leading to a more positive outlook (Beck, 2011).

Reframing is a technique that involves looking at a situation or thought from a different perspective. It's about finding the silver lining or the lesson in a challenging situation. For example, instead of thinking, "I failed at this task," you could reframe it as, "This task didn't go as planned, but I learned something valuable that I can use next time." Reframing helps shift our focus from the negative to the positive, fostering a more resilient mindset.

Mindfulness is the practice of being present in the moment and observing our thoughts and feelings without judgment. It allows us to become aware of our negative thought patterns and gently guide our attention back to the present moment. Mindfulness meditation, in particular, has been shown to reduce rumination and improve mood, making it an effective tool for transforming negative thoughts into positive ones (Keng et al., 2011).

Self-compassion involves treating ourselves with the same kindness and understanding that we would offer a friend. When we encounter negative thoughts, instead of being self-critical, we can practice self-compassion by acknowledging our feelings and reminding ourselves that we are not alone in our struggles. Research has shown that self-compassion can reduce negative emotions and enhance emotional well-being (Neff & Germer, 2013).

Cultivating gratitude is a powerful way to shift our focus from negative thoughts to positive ones. By regularly reflecting on the things we are thankful for, we can develop a more appreciative and optimistic mindset. Studies have found that gratitude is associated with greater happiness, reduced depression, and improved resilience (Emmons & McCullough, 2003).

Positive affirmations are statements that affirm our worth, strengths, and abilities. Repeating these affirmations can help reinforce positive beliefs and counteract negative thoughts. It's important to choose affirmations that resonate with you and reflect your values and goals.

Transforming negative thoughts into positive ones is a journey that requires patience, practice, and self-compassion. By employing techniques such as cognitive restructuring, reframing, mindfulness, self-compassion, gratitude, and positive affirmations, we can cultivate a more positive and resilient mindset. Embracing these strategies can lead to a life filled with greater joy, peace, and fulfillment.

Cultivating a Balanced and Positive Mindset

Amidst the whirlwind of life's challenges, cultivating a balanced and positive mindset is like finding a serene oasis in a desert. It's about nurturing a state of mind that remains hopeful and resilient, even when the storms of life rage on. This section delves into the importance of self-care, setting boundaries, and seeking support as pillars for preserving mental and emotional balance.

Self-care is the cornerstone of a balanced and positive mindset. It's the act of taking time to nurture yourself, both physically and emotionally. Engaging in regular self-care activities can replenish your energy, reduce stress, and enhance your overall well-being. Whether it's indulging in a relaxing bath, going for a walk in nature, practicing yoga, or simply enjoying a cup of tea, self-care is a personal and vital ritual that helps keep your inner balance intact.

Setting boundaries is crucial for maintaining a positive mindset. It's about knowing your limits and communicating them clearly to others. Boundaries help protect your energy and prevent burnout. They allow you to say no to things that drain you and yes to things that nourish you. By setting healthy boundaries, you honor your needs and create space for positivity to flourish.

No one is an island, and seeking support when needed is a sign of strength, not weakness. Whether it's confiding in a trusted friend, joining a support group, or seeking professional help, reaching out for support can provide comfort, guidance, and a fresh perspective. It's important to remember that you don't have to face life's challenges alone, and there is strength in vulnerability.

Cultivating gratitude is a powerful way to maintain a positive mindset. By focusing on the blessings in your life, you shift your attention away from negativity and towards abundance. Practicing gratitude can be as simple as keeping a gratitude journal, where you jot down things you're thankful for each day. This practice can increase happiness, reduce stress, and create a more positive outlook on life.

Mindfulness and positive affirmations are valuable tools for cultivating a balanced mindset. Mindfulness keeps you grounded in the present moment, reducing worry and anxiety. Positive affirmations, on the other hand, are uplifting statements that reinforce your strengths and capabilities. Together, mindfulness and affirmations can help you navigate life with grace and positivity.

A growth mindset is the belief that you can grow and learn through challenges. It's about embracing failures as opportunities for growth and viewing obstacles as stepping stones to success. Cultivating a growth mindset fosters resilience, encourages continuous learning, and contributes to a more balanced and positive outlook on life.

Cultivating a balanced and positive mindset is an ongoing journey that requires intention, effort, and self-compassion. By prioritizing self-care, setting boundaries, seeking support, practicing gratitude, embracing mindfulness, and nurturing a growth mindset, you can navigate life's challenges with greater ease and optimism. Remember, a balanced and positive mindset is not about denying the difficulties of life but about choosing to face them with hope, resilience, and a sense of inner peace.

References

- Bernstein, G. (2019). *Super Attractor: Methods for Manifesting a Life Beyond Your Wildest Dreams*. Hay House, Inc.
- Hay, L. L. (1984). *You Can Heal Your Life*. Hay House, Inc.
- Lipton, B. (2016). *The Biology of Belief: Unleashing the Power*

of Consciousness, Matter & Miracles. Hay House, Inc.

- Beck, J. S. (2011). *Cognitive Behavior Therapy: Basics and Beyond* (2nd ed.). Guilford Press.

- Emmons, R. A., & McCullough, M. E. (2003). Counting blessings versus burdens: An experimental investigation of gratitude and subjective well-being in daily life. *Journal of Personality and Social Psychology*, 84(2), 377-389.

- Keng, S. L., Smoski, M. J., & Robins, C. J. (2011). Effects of mindfulness on psychological health: A review of empirical studies. *Clinical Psychology Review*, 31(6), 1041-1056.

- Neff, K. D., & Germer, C. K. (2013). A pilot study and randomized controlled trial of the mindful self-compassion program. *Journal of Clinical Psychology*, 69(1), 28-44.

- • Kabat-Zinn, J. (1994). *Wherever You Go, There You Are: Mindfulness Meditation in Everyday Life*. Hyperion.

- • Neff, K. (2011). *Self-Compassion: The Proven Power of Being Kind to Yourself*. William Morrow.

- • Dweck, C. S. (2006). *Mindset: The New Psychology of Success*. Random House

****

Chapter 4

Anchoring in the Now:

The Importance of Present-Moment Awareness

Chuck, who was first mentioned in the Introduction of this book, is a devoted father and for most of his working life up to this moment in time, he had been a fairly successful financial analyst. When the recent economic downturn began to suggest his job was at risk, Chuck began to feel his stress levels rise to new thresholds. Chuck was struggling to maintain a sense of calm amidst the uncertainty. The stress of potentially losing his income while supporting his family has made it challenging for him to find peace and balance in his life.

Chuck's days of worrying, and coping with life-sucking stress went on for days and even weeks, but not months, for soon his worse fear came true. His office was downsized, and Chuck was one of the many let go.

At age 52, Chuck found himself pulling together a resume, and going door to door, lining up interviews, or even a chance to speak on the phone. Jobs were scare in his field of expertise, and for weeks Chuck went to every potential employer telling them how good he had been at his job in the past. It didn't take long for Chuck to notice how he was being side-passed for 20 year olds with little to no experience.

One night, as Chuck sat at a bar, a man came and sat beside him. "It's Chuck isn't it?" Chuck looked over not recognizing the man.

"I remember you coming in for an interview. You had an excellent resume and work history." The man was being genuine in his comments to Chuck.

"Well, not good enough to get the job..." Chuck was grumbling, "...but that's water under the bridge. I was the best at what I did, but it simply wasn't enough. Now all they want are the inexperienced 20 year olds."

The man looked at Chuck for a moment before speaking. "Chuck, you really were the best at what you did. It's sad that your last company did not stay current with industry software. Now, most companies have replaced phone lines with computer lines. You really were the best with the phone lines. Sadly, you're losing out today to 20 year olds who are good with software and computers." The man paused for a minute and stared at how Chuck was reacting. "I only have a minute here, Chuck, I would encourage you to not focus on what you were in the past, but focus on what you are in the present, that might help you understand what needs to change for you to be more recruitable. Focus on being more present minded."

In a world that often pulls us in multiple directions, it's easy to lose sight of the here and now. Yet, as Lao Tzu wisely said, "If you are depressed, you are living in the past. If you are anxious, you are living in the future. If you are at peace, you are living in the present." This chapter explores the essence of present-moment awareness and its profound impact on our well-being.

Being present means fully engaging with the current moment, with an open and non-judgmental attitude. It's about experiencing life as it unfolds, without being preoccupied with past regrets or future worries. Present-moment awareness invites us to savor the richness of life, whether we're enjoying a beautiful sunset, sharing a meal with loved ones, or even navigating challenging situations.

Our minds have a tendency to wander, often dwelling on past experiences or future uncertainties. While reflection and planning are natural and necessary aspects of life, excessive rumination can lead to stress and anxiety. By anchoring ourselves in the present, we can alleviate these worries and cultivate a sense of peace and clarity.

Living in the present offers numerous benefits for our mental, emotional, and physical well-being. It allows us to fully experience and appreciate life, leading to increased happiness and gratitude. Present-moment awareness also enhances our relationships, as we become more attentive and connected to those around us. Moreover, it improves our resilience, enabling us to navigate life's challenges with greater ease and equanimity.

Cultivating present-moment awareness is a practice that requires intention and effort. Techniques such as mindfulness meditation, deep breathing, and mindful observation can help us develop this skill. By integrating these practices into our daily lives, we can learn to stay present and grounded, even in the midst of chaos.

Embracing present-moment awareness is a journey that unfolds over time. It's a path that invites us to slow down, savor the moment, and embrace the fullness of life. As Jon Kabat-Zinn, a pioneer in the field of mindfulness, reminds us, "The best way to capture moments is to pay attention. This is how we cultivate mindfulness." By anchoring in the now, we open ourselves to a world of beauty, connection, and peace.

As we explore the importance of present-moment awareness in this chapter, we invite you to embark on this journey with us. Together, we'll discover how to anchor ourselves in the now, transforming our lives one moment at a time.

Defining Present-Moment Awareness

In the fast-paced world we live in, it's easy to get caught up in the whirlwind of daily activities, future plans, and past reflections. However, there's a profound beauty and peace in embracing the present moment, a concept that is at the heart of mindfulness. Present-moment awareness is more than just being physically present; it's about being mentally and emotionally engaged in the here and now.

Being present means fully experiencing the moment you are in, with all your senses and without judgment. It's about noticing the details of your environment, the sensations in your body, and the thoughts and emotions that arise. Present-moment awareness is the opposite of autopilot mode, where we go through the motions of life without truly experiencing them.

Mindfulness is a practice that helps cultivate present-moment awareness. It involves paying attention to the present moment with openness, curiosity, and acceptance. Mindfulness can be practiced through formal meditation or informally by bringing a mindful attitude to everyday activities.

Jon Kabat-Zinn, a pioneer in the field of mindfulness, defines it as "paying attention in a particular way: on purpose, in the present moment, and nonjudgmentally" (Kabat-Zinn, 1994). This definition highlights the intentional and nonjudgmental aspects of mindfulness, which are key to cultivating present-moment awareness.

Living in the present moment has numerous benefits for our mental, emotional, and physical well-being. It can reduce stress and anxiety by preventing rumination on the past or worry about the future. It can enhance enjoyment and appreciation of life by allowing us to fully engage with our experiences. It can improve relationships by fostering deeper connections and communication. Finally, it can increase resilience by helping us respond to challenges with clarity and calmness.

Practical Ways to Cultivate Present-Moment Awareness

Cultivating present-moment awareness is a practice that can be integrated into daily life. Here are some practical ways to foster this mindset:

- **Mindful Breathing**: Take a few moments to focus on your breath, noticing the sensations of inhaling and exhaling.
- **Mindful Observation**: Choose an object and observe it with full attention, noticing its colors, textures, and details.
- **Mindful Listening**: Listen to the sounds around you without labeling or judging them, simply experiencing them as they are.
- **Mindful Eating**: Eat slowly and savor the flavors, textures, and smells of your food.
- **Mindful Walking**: Pay attention to the sensations of your feet touching the ground and the sights and sounds around you as you walk.

Overcoming Challenges to Present-Moment Awareness

Staying present is not always easy, especially in a world filled with distractions. Common challenges include:

- **Mind Wandering**: Our minds naturally wander, and it's normal for thoughts to drift away from the present moment. The key is to gently bring your attention back without self-criticism.
- **Emotional Discomfort**: Being present means facing our emotions, including the uncomfortable ones. It's important to approach these feelings with compassion and curiosity.
- **External Distractions**: Technology, noise, and other external factors can pull us away from the present moment. Setting boundaries and creating a conducive environment can help

mitigate these distractions.

Defining present-moment awareness is about recognizing the richness of the here and now. By embracing mindfulness, we can cultivate a deeper sense of presence, leading to a more fulfilling and balanced life. As we navigate the journey of present-moment awareness, we learn to appreciate the beauty of each moment and the peace that comes with truly being anchored in the now.

The Impact of Dwelling on the Past and Future

In the tapestry of life, our thoughts are the threads that weave the fabric of our experiences. Dwelling on the past and future, however, can entangle us in a web of stress and anxiety, detracting from the beauty of the present moment. This chapter explores the impact of rumination and worry on our well-being and highlights how present-moment awareness can serve as a liberating antidote.

Our minds have a natural tendency to wander through time. Memories of the past and anticipations of the future often dominate our thoughts, leaving little room for the present. While reflecting on the past and planning for the future are essential aspects of being human, excessive rumination and worry can become detrimental to our mental and emotional health.

When we dwell on past events, especially negative ones, we may experience feelings of regret, guilt, or sadness. This backward-looking focus can lead to a cycle of negative thinking that is hard to break. Similarly, worrying about the future can create a sense of uncertainty and fear, making us feel anxious and overwhelmed. This forward-looking focus can paralyze us, preventing us from taking action or enjoying the present.

Present-moment awareness, or mindfulness, is a powerful tool for breaking free from the cycle of rumination and worry. By anchoring ourselves in the present, we can observe our thoughts and emotions without getting swept away by them. This detachment allows us to respond to life's challenges with clarity and wisdom, rather than reacting impulsively or defensively.

Practicing mindfulness can help us cultivate present-moment awareness. Simple practices like mindful breathing, mindful walking, and mindful eating can train our minds to focus on the here and now. Over time, these practices can transform our relationship with time, enabling us to savor the richness of each moment.

Living in the present moment has numerous benefits for our well-being. It can reduce stress and anxiety, enhance our emotional resilience, and improve our overall quality of life. When we are fully present, we are more likely to experience joy, gratitude, and a deep sense of connection with ourselves and the world around us.

Several barriers can impede our ability to live in the present moment, including habitual patterns of thinking, external distractions, and resistance to change. Overcoming these barriers requires patience, persistence, and a gentle, non-judgmental attitude toward ourselves.

The impact of dwelling on the past and future is profound, yet present-moment awareness offers a path to liberation. By embracing the present, we can free ourselves from the chains of stress and anxiety and open the door to a more peaceful and fulfilling life.

Benefits of Living in the Present

Embracing the present moment is akin to opening a treasure chest filled with invaluable gems. Present-moment awareness, or mindfulness, is not merely a practice but a way of life that offers a plethora of benefits. It is a gentle reminder to live life fully, one moment at a time. This section delves into the various benefits of living in the present, supported by psychological research.

One of the most significant benefits of living in the present is the reduction of stress and anxiety. When we focus on the here and now, we are less likely to ruminate on past events or worry about future uncertainties. Research has shown that mindfulness-based interventions can significantly reduce symptoms of stress and anxiety (Hofmann et al., 2010). By anchoring ourselves in the present, we can navigate life's challenges with greater ease and tranquility.

Present-moment awareness enhances our ability to regulate our emotions. It allows us to observe our feelings without being overwhelmed by them. Studies have demonstrated that mindfulness can improve emotional regulation, leading to better mood and increased resilience (Teper et al., 2013). When we are mindful, we can respond to situations with clarity and wisdom, rather than reacting impulsively.

Living in the present can also enrich our relationships. When we are fully present with others, we can listen more attentively, communicate more effectively, and connect more deeply. Mindfulness can foster empathy and compassion, which are essential for building strong, meaningful relationships. Research has shown that couples who practice mindfulness report higher levels of relationship satisfaction (Carson et al., 2004).

Embracing the present moment can lead to greater overall well-being. It can increase life satisfaction, boost happiness, and enhance our sense of gratitude. Mindfulness has been associated with improved physical health, including lower blood pressure, better sleep, and a stronger immune system (Black & Slavich, 2016). By living in the present, we can cultivate a sense of joy and contentment that permeates all aspects of our lives.

Present-moment awareness can improve our focus and productivity. When we are mindful, we can concentrate more fully on the task at hand, leading to better performance and efficiency. Studies have shown that mindfulness training can enhance cognitive function, including attention and memory (Jha et al., 2007). By being present, we can achieve more with less effort and stress.

Living in the present offers a myriad of benefits that can transform our lives. It reduces stress and anxiety, improves emotional regulation, enhances relationships, and promotes overall well-being. By cultivating present-moment awareness, we can navigate life's journey with grace, joy, and a deep sense of fulfillment.

Practical Techniques for Cultivating Present-Moment Awareness

Cultivating present-moment awareness is a journey that can transform our lives, bringing a sense of peace, clarity, and joy to our everyday experiences. This section offers practical techniques to help you develop the ability to stay present, providing step-by-step guidance for integrating these practices into your daily life.

Mindfulness meditation is a cornerstone practice for cultivating present-moment awareness. It involves sitting quietly and focusing your attention on your breath or a chosen object of meditation. Here's a simple guide to get started:

1. **Find a Quiet Space**: Choose a quiet place where you can sit comfortably without distractions.
2. **Set a Time Limit**: Start with a short period, such as 5-10 minutes, and gradually increase as you become more

comfortable with the practice.

3. **Focus on Your Breath**: Close your eyes and bring your attention to your breath. Notice the sensation of the air entering and leaving your nostrils or the rise and fall of your chest.

4. **Return to Your Breath**: When your mind wanders, gently acknowledge the distraction and bring your focus back to your breath.

Deep breathing is a simple yet effective technique for calming the mind and staying present. Here's how to practice deep breathing:

1. **Find a Comfortable Position**: Sit or lie down in a comfortable position, with your hands on your abdomen.

2. **Breathe Deeply**: Slowly inhale through your nose, feeling your abdomen expand. Then, exhale slowly through your mouth or nose, feeling your abdomen contract.

3. **Focus on Your Breath**: Pay attention to the sensation of your breath as you inhale and exhale. If your mind wanders, gently bring your attention back to your breath.

A body scan is a mindfulness practice that involves paying attention to different parts of your body in a systematic way. Here's a guide to performing a body scan:

1. **Lie Down**: Lie on your back in a comfortable position, with your arms at your sides and your palms facing up.

2. **Start with Your Feet**: Bring your attention to your feet, noticing any sensations or tension. Breathe into any areas of discomfort and release tension as you exhale.

3. **Move Up Your Body**: Gradually move your attention up your body, from your feet to your legs, abdomen, chest, arms, and head. Take your time and focus on each area with

curiosity and openness.

Mindful listening is a practice that involves fully engaging with the sounds around you. Here's how to practice mindful listening:

1. **Find a Quiet Place**: Choose a quiet place where you can sit comfortably and listen to the sounds around you.
2. **Listen Attentively**: Close your eyes and listen to the sounds in your environment. Notice the different qualities of each sound, such as pitch, volume, and duration.
3. **Observe Your Reactions**: Pay attention to any thoughts or emotions that arise as you listen. Acknowledge them without judgment and return your focus to the sounds.

You can cultivate present-moment awareness by bringing mindfulness to everyday activities. Here are some suggestions:

- **Mindful Eating**: Pay attention to the flavors, textures, and sensations of your food as you eat.
- **Mindful Walking**: Focus on the sensation of your feet touching the ground as you walk.
- **Mindful Communication**: Listen attentively when speaking with others, and speak with intention and kindness.

Cultivating present-moment awareness is a practice that can enrich your life in countless ways. By integrating mindfulness meditation, deep breathing exercises, body scans, mindful listening, and mindfulness into daily activities, you can develop a deeper connection to the present moment and experience life with greater clarity, peace, and joy.

Overcoming Challenges to Present-Moment Awareness

Staying present in the moment can be a challenge in our fast-paced, distraction-filled world. The path to present-moment awareness is often strewn with obstacles such as distractions, mental chatter, and emotional discomfort. However, with mindfulness and self-compassion, we can navigate these challenges and cultivate a deeper sense of presence. This section explores common obstacles to staying present and offers tips for overcoming them.

One of the most common obstacles to present-moment awareness is distractions. Our environment is filled with stimuli vying for our attention, from the ping of a new email to the buzz of a smartphone. To counteract these distractions, it's essential to create a conducive environment for mindfulness. This might involve setting aside specific times for mindfulness practice, turning off electronic devices, or finding a quiet space where you can focus without interruptions.

Our minds are often filled with a constant stream of thoughts, memories, and worries. This mental chatter can make it difficult to stay present. To quiet the noise, try focusing your attention on a single point, such as your breath or a mantra. When you notice your mind wandering, gently redirect your attention back to your chosen focus. With practice, you'll find it easier to quiet the mental chatter and stay present.

Staying present also means being with our emotions, including the uncomfortable ones. Emotional discomfort can be a significant barrier to present-moment awareness, as we may try to avoid or suppress our feelings. However, mindfulness teaches us to observe our emotions without judgment or attachment. By acknowledging and accepting our emotions, we can navigate them with greater ease and find peace in the present moment.

Life can present us with challenging situations that test our ability to stay present. In these moments, it's crucial to lean on your mindfulness practice. Remind yourself that you can only control your response to the situation, not the situation itself. Use mindfulness techniques, such as deep breathing or grounding exercises, to center yourself and approach the challenge with clarity and calm.

Self-compassion is a powerful ally in overcoming obstacles to present-moment awareness. It involves treating yourself with the same kindness and understanding that you would offer a friend. When you encounter challenges in staying present, practice self-compassion by acknowledging your efforts and reminding yourself that it's okay to be imperfect.

Overcoming challenges to present-moment awareness is an ongoing journey. By recognizing and addressing common obstacles such as distractions, mental chatter, and emotional discomfort, we can cultivate a deeper sense of presence and live more fully in each moment. With mindfulness and self-compassion as our guides, we can navigate the challenges of life with grace and ease.

References

- Kabat-Zinn, J. (1994). *Wherever You Go, There You Are: Mindfulness Meditation in Everyday Life*. Hyperion.
- Tzu, L. (n.d.). *Tao Te Ching*.
- Nolen-Hoeksema, S. (2008). *Rumination and Worry as Mediators of the Relationship Between Self-Compassion and Depression and Anxiety*. Mindfulness, 1(2), 140-150.
- Thich Nhat Hanh. (1991). *The Miracle of Mindfulness: An Introduction to the Practice of Meditation*. Beacon Press. Black, D. S., & Slavich, G. M. (2016). Mindfulness meditation and the immune system: a systematic review of randomized controlled trials. *Annals of the New York Academy of Sciences,*

1373(1), 13-24.

- Carson, J. W., Carson, K. M., Gil, K. M., & Baucom, D. H. (2004). Mindfulness-based relationship enhancement. *Behavior Therapy*, 35(3), 471-494.

- Hofmann, S. G., Sawyer, A. T., Witt, A. A., & Oh, D. (2010). The effect of mindfulness-based therapy on anxiety and depression: A meta-analytic review. *Journal of Consulting and Clinical Psychology*, 78(2), 169-183.

- Jha, A. P., Krompinger, J., & Baime, M. J. (2007). Mindfulness training modifies subsystems of attention. *Cognitive, Affective, & Behavioral Neuroscience*, 7(2), 109-119.

- Teper, R., Segal, Z. V., & Inzlicht, M. (2013). Inside the mindful mind: How mindfulness enhances emotion regulation through improvements in executive control. *Current Directions in Psychological Science*, 22(6), 449-454.

- Neff, K. D. (2011). *Self-Compassion: The Proven Power of Being Kind to Yourself*. William Morrow.

****

Chapter 5

Sailing Through Self-Talk:

Reframing Your Inner Dialogue

In the chapter titled "Sailing Through Self-Talk: Reframing Your Inner Dialogue," we embark on a journey to explore the profound impact of our inner dialogue on our lives. Self-talk, the ongoing conversation we have with ourselves, can be a powerful force, shaping our perceptions, emotions, and behaviors. It's the voice that narrates our life's story, and learning to master it can lead us to greater confidence and resilience.

Our voyage begins with the crucial task of identifying negative self-talk. This form of inner dialogue can be a subtle saboteur, undermining our confidence with self-critical thoughts, catastrophic predictions, and other unhelpful patterns. Recognizing these negative voices is the first step toward transformation. As we become more aware of the ways we speak to ourselves, we can start to challenge and change these patterns.

Once we've identified negative self-talk, the next step is to challenge and reframe these thoughts. This involves examining the evidence for and against our negative beliefs and replacing them with more constructive, empowering statements. By questioning the validity of our negative thoughts, we can begin to see ourselves and our situations in a more positive light.

Cultivating positive self-talk is an ongoing practice that requires intentionality and commitment. It's about nurturing an inner dialogue that supports and empowers us. This can be achieved through affirmations, gratitude practices, and focusing on our strengths and achievements. By consciously choosing positive words and phrases, we can shift our mindset and foster a more optimistic outlook on life.

Mindfulness plays a pivotal role in transforming our self-talk. It's the art of being present and fully engaged in the moment, without judgment. Mindfulness allows us to observe our thoughts and feelings without getting caught up in them. By practicing mindfulness, we can develop the ability to choose how we respond to our inner dialogue, selecting thoughts that serve us well.

The true test of our mastery over self-talk comes in applying it to everyday situations. Whether it's in our work, relationships, or personal growth, positive self-talk can be a powerful tool for navigating life's challenges. This section provides practical examples and exercises for using positive self-talk in various aspects of life, helping us to sail through our days with greater ease and confidence.

By sailing through our self-talk and reframing our inner dialogue, we can empower ourselves to navigate life's challenges with greater confidence and resilience. It's a journey that requires patience, practice, and self-compassion, but the rewards are immeasurable. As we learn to master our self-talk, we can chart a course toward a more fulfilling and empowered life.

Identifying Negative Self-Talk

The journey to a healthier, more positive mindset begins with identifying negative self-talk. This internal dialogue can shape our perceptions and influence our emotions and behaviors in profound ways. By becoming aware of the patterns of our self-talk, we can start to challenge and transform them, paving the way for a more empowered and optimistic outlook on life.

Self-talk is the inner voice that narrates our thoughts and feelings throughout the day. It's the running commentary that interprets our experiences and guides our actions. While self-talk can be positive and supportive, it often veers into negative territory, leading to feelings of doubt, fear, and limitation.

Negative self-talk can take many forms, each with its own impact on our well-being:

- **Self-Critical Thoughts**: These are thoughts that focus on our perceived flaws and shortcomings, such as "I'm not good enough" or "I always mess things up." They can erode our self-esteem and hinder our growth.
- **Catastrophic Thinking**: This involves imagining the worst possible outcomes, such as "If I fail this exam, my life is over." It can amplify our anxiety and prevent us from taking risks.
- **Overgeneralization**: This is when we take one negative event and generalize it to our entire life, such as "I didn't get the job, so I'll never be successful." It can create a sense of hopelessness and defeat.
- **Mind Reading**: This involves assuming we know what others are thinking, often negatively, such as "They must think I'm incompetent." It can lead to misunderstandings and strained relationships.
- **Should Statements**: These are thoughts that impose unrealistic expectations on ourselves, such as "I should always be happy" or "I should never make mistakes." They can create unnecessary pressure and guilt.

Negative self-talk can have a profound impact on our mental and emotional well-being. It can:

- Increase stress and anxiety by focusing on fears and worst-case scenarios.
- Lower self-esteem by reinforcing feelings of inadequacy and unworthiness.
- Hinder decision-making by clouding our judgment with doubt and negativity.
- Strain relationships by fostering miscommunication and resentment.

To transform our self-talk, we first need to become adept at identifying negative patterns. Here are some strategies to help:

- **Mindfulness**: Practice mindfulness to become more aware of your thoughts and feelings. Pay attention to your inner dialogue without judgment.
- **Journaling**: Keep a journal to record your thoughts and emotions. Look for patterns of negative self-talk that recur over time.
- **Reflection**: Take time to reflect on your day and the thoughts that dominated your mind. Consider how these thoughts affected your mood and behavior.
- **Feedback**: Seek feedback from trusted friends or family members about how they perceive your self-talk. They may offer valuable insights into patterns you're not aware of.

Identifying negative self-talk is the first crucial step toward cultivating a more positive and supportive inner dialogue. By becoming aware of the ways in which we talk to ourselves, we can begin to challenge and change these patterns, leading to a more empowered and fulfilling life.

Challenging and Reframing Negative Thoughts

Once we've identified our negative self-talk, the next crucial step is to challenge and reframe these thoughts into more positive, constructive ones. This process involves questioning the validity of our negative beliefs and replacing them with empowering statements that reflect a more balanced and optimistic perspective.

Reframing is a cognitive-behavioral technique that involves changing the way we interpret events and situations. By altering our perspective, we can shift our emotional and behavioral responses. This is particularly powerful in dealing with negative self-talk, as it allows us to transform self-defeating thoughts into ones that support our growth and well-being.

Challenging negative thoughts involves examining the evidence for and against our beliefs. It's about asking ourselves questions like:

- "Is this thought based on facts or assumptions?"
- "Are there alternative explanations or perspectives I haven't considered?"
- "What would I say to a friend who had this thought?"

By scrutinizing our negative thoughts, we can uncover distortions and inaccuracies, paving the way for a more balanced mindset.

Reframing negative thoughts requires creativity and practice. Here are some techniques to help you get started:

- **Look for the Silver Lining**: Try to find something positive in every situation, no matter how small.
- **Use Positive Language**: Replace negative words with positive ones. For example, instead of saying "I can't handle this," say "I can cope with this challenge."
- **Focus on Solutions**: Shift your focus from the problem to potential solutions. Ask yourself, "What can I do to improve

this situation?"

- **Practice Gratitude**: Cultivate an attitude of gratitude by focusing on what you're thankful for in your life.
- **Visualize Success**: Imagine yourself succeeding and overcoming your challenges. Visualization can be a powerful motivator.

Mindfulness plays a crucial role in the process of reframing. By staying present and observing our thoughts without judgment, we can gain the clarity and insight needed to challenge and reframe them. Mindfulness helps us to detach from our negative thoughts and see them for what they are: just thoughts, not facts.

To make reframing a part of your daily life, it's important to practice regularly. Start by focusing on one negative thought at a time and work on reframing it. As you become more skilled at this process, you'll find it easier to apply it to other areas of your life.

Challenging and reframing negative thoughts is a powerful tool for transforming our inner dialogue. By questioning the validity of our negative beliefs and replacing them with positive, empowering statements, we can cultivate a more optimistic and resilient mindset. Remember, the way we talk to ourselves shapes our reality, so let's choose words that uplift and inspire us.

Cultivating Positive Self-Talk

In the garden of our minds, self-talk is the seed from which our thoughts and beliefs grow. Cultivating positive self-talk is akin to nurturing a garden, requiring practice, intentionality, and care. It's about sowing seeds of affirmation, gratitude, and self-appreciation that can blossom into a more optimistic and empowered mindset.

Positive self-talk is a transformative tool that can reshape our inner dialogue, influencing our emotions, behaviors, and overall well-being. It's the gentle voice that encourages us, the compassionate voice that forgives us, and the hopeful voice that believes in us. By fostering positive self-talk, we can build self-esteem, reduce stress, and create a more fulfilling life.

Affirmations are positive statements that can help reinforce our self-worth and goals. They are a powerful way to practice positive self-talk, as they allow us to assert our values and aspirations. Crafting personal affirmations involves choosing words that resonate with our deepest desires and repeating them regularly. For example, "I am capable of achieving my dreams" or "I am worthy of love and respect."

Gratitude is a cornerstone of positive self-talk. It shifts our focus from what we lack to what we have, fostering a sense of abundance and contentment. Practicing gratitude can be as simple as keeping a gratitude journal, where we jot down things we're thankful for each day. This practice helps us appreciate the small joys and blessings in our lives, reinforcing a positive mindset.

Recognizing our strengths and achievements is crucial for developing positive self-talk. It's about acknowledging our talents, celebrating our successes, and learning from our experiences. By focusing on our positive attributes, we can build confidence and resilience. It's important to remind ourselves of our accomplishments, no matter how small, and to recognize the progress we've made.

Mindfulness plays a vital role in cultivating positive self-talk. It allows us to observe our thoughts without judgment, giving us the space to choose how we respond to them. By practicing mindfulness, we can become more aware of our negative self-talk and consciously shift it towards a more positive and supportive dialogue.

Cultivating positive self-talk is a journey with its ups and downs. It's normal to encounter challenges, such as ingrained negative thought patterns or external criticism. The key is to be patient and compassionate with ourselves, recognizing that change takes time. It's also helpful to surround ourselves with supportive people who uplift and encourage us.

Cultivating positive self-talk is an act of self-love and empowerment. It's about nurturing a kind and encouraging inner voice that supports our growth and well-being. By practicing affirmations, gratitude, and mindfulness, and focusing on our strengths and achievements, we can transform our self-talk and, in turn, transform our lives.

Mindfulness and Self-Talk

In the intricate dance of the mind, mindfulness and self-talk play pivotal roles. Mindfulness, the art of being present and fully engaged in the moment, offers a lens through which we can observe our self-talk without judgment. This observation allows us to choose a more positive and supportive inner dialogue, leading to a healthier and more fulfilling life.

Mindfulness is the practice of bringing our full attention to the present moment, with openness, curiosity, and acceptance. It's about noticing our thoughts, feelings, and sensations as they arise, without getting caught up in them. Mindfulness helps us become aware of our habitual thought patterns, including our self-talk.

Our self-talk is often automatic and can be influenced by past experiences, beliefs, and emotions. Mindfulness allows us to step back and observe this self-talk from a distance. By doing so, we can recognize when our inner dialogue is negative or self-defeating and choose to respond in a more positive and compassionate way.

One of the key aspects of mindfulness is non-judgmental observation. When we listen to our self-talk without judgment, we create space for understanding and change. Instead of criticizing ourselves for negative thoughts, we can approach them with curiosity and kindness, exploring their origins and their impact on our well-being.

With mindfulness, we have the power to choose our inner dialogue. Instead of being swept away by negative self-talk, we can consciously decide to focus on positive, affirming thoughts. This shift in focus can have a profound impact on our emotions, behaviors, and overall quality of life.

There are several mindfulness practices that can help us transform our self-talk:

- **Mindful Breathing**: By focusing on our breath, we can anchor ourselves in the present moment and observe our thoughts with greater clarity.
- **Body Scan**: This practice involves paying attention to each part of the body, which can help us become more aware of the physical sensations associated with our thoughts.
- **Loving-Kindness Meditation**: This form of meditation involves sending wishes of love and kindness to ourselves and others, fostering a more positive and compassionate inner dialogue.

Cultivating mindful self-talk offers numerous benefits, including:

- **Reduced Stress and Anxiety**: By breaking the cycle of negative self-talk, we can reduce feelings of stress and anxiety.
- **Increased Self-Esteem**: Positive self-talk can boost our confidence and self-worth.
- **Improved Decision-Making**: With a clearer and more

positive mindset, we can make better decisions.

- **Enhanced Relationships**: Mindful self-talk can improve our communication and deepen our connections with others.

Transforming our self-talk through mindfulness is a journey that requires patience and persistence. We may encounter challenges, such as deeply ingrained negative thought patterns or resistance to change. It's important to approach these challenges with self-compassion and to remember that change takes time.

Mindfulness and self-talk are intimately connected, each influencing the other. By practicing mindfulness, we can observe our self-talk without judgment and choose a more positive and supportive inner dialogue. This shift in self-talk can lead to greater well-being, resilience, and joy in our lives.

Self-Talk in Action: Applying Positive Self-Talk in Everyday Situations

Positive self-talk is not just a concept to be understood, but a practice to be lived. It's about integrating this empowering inner dialogue into every aspect of our lives, from work to relationships to personal growth. In this section, we'll explore practical examples and exercises for using positive self-talk in various everyday situations.

Work can be a significant source of stress, but positive self-talk can help us navigate professional challenges with confidence and resilience. For example, before a big presentation, instead of thinking, "I'm going to mess this up," you can tell yourself, "I am prepared and capable of delivering a great presentation." When faced with criticism or feedback, instead of internalizing it as a personal failure, reframe it as an opportunity for growth: "This feedback is valuable and will help me improve."

Positive self-talk can also enhance our relationships. It can help us communicate more effectively, empathize with others, and maintain a healthy perspective during conflicts. For instance, if you're feeling upset after an argument with a partner, instead of ruminating on negative thoughts like "They don't care about me," try to shift your focus to more constructive thoughts like "We both need some time to cool off, and then we can work through this together."

Personal growth is an ongoing journey, and positive self-talk can be a powerful ally in this process. When pursuing a new goal or facing a personal challenge, encourage yourself with affirmations like "I am capable of achieving my goals" or "I am strong enough to overcome this obstacle." Celebrate your progress and achievements, no matter how small, and remind yourself of your strengths and potential.

Fear and anxiety are natural emotions, but they can be managed with positive self-talk. When faced with a situation that triggers fear, such as public speaking or trying something new, reassure yourself with thoughts like "I can handle this" or "I am brave enough to face this challenge." Focus on the present moment and remind yourself that you are safe and capable.

Positive self-talk is crucial for building and maintaining healthy self-esteem. Regularly affirm your worth and value with statements like "I am worthy of love and respect" and "I deserve happiness and success." Recognize and appreciate your unique qualities and contributions, and treat yourself with kindness and compassion.

Exercises for Practicing Positive Self-Talk

1. **Affirmation Journaling**: Start each day by writing down a

few positive affirmations that resonate with you. Repeat these affirmations throughout the day to reinforce positive self-talk.

2. **Mindfulness Meditation**: Incorporate mindfulness meditation into your routine to become more aware of your thoughts and practice observing them without judgment.
3. **Gratitude Practice**: End each day by reflecting on three things you're grateful for. This can shift your focus from negative thoughts to positive aspects of your life.
4. **Thought Replacement Exercise**: Whenever you catch yourself engaging in negative self-talk, consciously replace the negative thought with a positive one.
5. **Self-Compassion Breaks**: Take short breaks throughout the day to practice self-compassion. Speak to yourself as you would to a dear friend, offering words of encouragement and support.

Applying positive self-talk in everyday situations is a transformative practice that can lead to greater well-being, resilience, and fulfillment. By integrating these strategies into your daily life, you can cultivate a more positive and supportive inner dialogue that empowers you to navigate life's challenges with grace and confidence.

References

- Burns, D. D. (1999). *The Feeling Good Handbook*. Plume.
- Salzberg, S. (1995). *Loving-Kindness: The Revolutionary Art of Happiness*. Shambhala Publications.
- Seligman, M. E. P. (2002). *Authentic Happiness: Using the New Positive Psychology to Realize Your Potential for Lasting Fulfillment*. Free Press.

- Emmons, R. A., & McCullough, M. E. (2003). Counting blessings versus burdens: An experimental investigation of gratitude and subjective well-being in daily life. *Journal of Personality and Social Psychology*, 84(2), 377-389.
- Neff, K. D. (2011). *Self-Compassion: The Proven Power of Being Kind to Yourself*. William Morrow.
- Kabat-Zinn, J. (1994). *Wherever You Go, There You Are: Mindfulness Meditation in Everyday Life*. Hyperion.
- Beck, J. S. (2011). *Cognitive Behavior Therapy: Basics and Beyond* (2nd ed.). Guilford Press.

****

Chapter 6

Balancing the Ship:

Achieving Emotional and Mental Equilibrium

In the chapter titled "Balancing the Ship: Achieving Emotional and Mental Equilibrium," we delve into the art of finding balance amidst life's ups and downs, with a particular focus on emotional regulation. Achieving a state of equilibrium is akin to a ship maintaining its balance on the high seas; it requires skill, awareness, and the right tools.

Emotional regulation and emotional maturity are two pillars that support our mental and emotional balance. While they are interconnected, each plays a distinct role in how we navigate our inner world and our interactions with others.

Emotional regulation refers to our ability to manage and respond to our emotions in a healthy and adaptive manner. It involves recognizing our emotional states, understanding their triggers, and choosing appropriate ways to express and act on them. Emotional regulation is about maintaining control over our emotions, rather than letting them control us.

For example, when faced with a stressful situation at work, emotional regulation allows us to take a deep breath, assess the problem calmly, and respond in a constructive manner, rather than reacting impulsively with anger or frustration.

Emotional maturity, on the other hand, is a broader concept that encompasses not only the regulation of emotions but also the development of emotional wisdom and understanding. It involves recognizing and accepting our emotions, empathizing with others, and maintaining emotional stability even in challenging situations. Emotional maturity is about growing in emotional depth and complexity, allowing us to navigate life's ups and downs with grace and resilience.

For instance, someone who has reached a high level of emotional maturity is able to empathize with others' feelings, maintain composure in the face of adversity, and make decisions that consider both logical and emotional aspects.

While emotional regulation focuses on managing our emotions, emotional maturity involves a deeper understanding and acceptance of those emotions. Emotional regulation is often a stepping stone to emotional maturity, as it provides the tools needed to navigate our emotions effectively. As we become more adept at regulating our emotions, we can deepen our emotional maturity, leading to richer and more fulfilling relationships with ourselves and others.

Both emotional regulation and emotional maturity are crucial for achieving mental and emotional balance. They enable us to handle stress, build strong relationships, and lead a life that is aligned with our values and goals. By cultivating these skills, we can enhance our well-being and navigate life's challenges with greater ease and confidence.

Developing emotional regulation and emotional maturity takes time, practice, and self-reflection. Mindfulness practices, therapy, and self-help resources can be valuable tools in this journey. By investing in our emotional growth, we can build a solid foundation for a balanced and fulfilling life.

Understanding emotional regulation and emotional maturity is essential for anyone seeking to achieve mental and emotional balance.

While they are distinct concepts, they are deeply interconnected and mutually supportive. By cultivating both, we can navigate our emotions with wisdom and grace, leading to a more balanced and fulfilling life.

Techniques for Developing Emotional Regulation and Emotional Maturity

Emotional regulation and emotional maturity are essential skills for navigating the complexities of life with grace and resilience. Developing these skills involves a combination of self-awareness, practice, and intentionality. Here, we explore various techniques that can help individuals cultivate emotional regulation and emotional maturity.

Mindfulness is a foundational practice for developing both emotional regulation and emotional maturity. It involves paying attention to the present moment with openness, curiosity, and acceptance. By practicing mindfulness, individuals can become more aware of their emotions, thoughts, and bodily sensations, allowing them to respond to situations with greater clarity and intention.

- **Mindful Breathing**: Taking slow, deep breaths can help calm the mind and body, making it easier to regulate emotions.
- **Body Scan Meditation**: This practice involves paying attention to different parts of the body, noticing any sensations or emotions that arise, and accepting them without judgment.
- **Mindful Observation**: Engaging in mindful observation of one's surroundings can help anchor individuals in the present moment, reducing the impact of negative thoughts or emotions.

Cognitive-behavioral techniques are effective in challenging and changing unhelpful thought patterns that contribute to emotional dysregulation.

- **Thought Challenging**: This involves identifying negative thoughts, evaluating their accuracy, and replacing them with more balanced and realistic thoughts.
- **Reframing**: Reframing is a technique used to change the way individuals perceive a situation, which can, in turn, change their emotional response.
- **Behavioral Activation**: Engaging in activities that bring joy and fulfillment can help improve mood and emotional well-being.

Emotional intelligence is the ability to understand and manage one's own emotions as well as the emotions of others. Developing emotional intelligence is key to emotional maturity.

- **Self-Reflection**: Regular self-reflection can help individuals understand their emotional patterns, triggers, and responses.
- **Empathy Practice**: Practicing empathy, or the ability to understand and share the feelings of others, can enhance emotional maturity and improve relationships.
- **Effective Communication**: Learning to express emotions in a clear and assertive manner can lead to healthier interactions and emotional balance.

Effective stress management is crucial for emotional regulation. Engaging in relaxation techniques can help reduce stress and promote emotional stability.

- **Progressive Muscle Relaxation**: This technique involves tensing and then relaxing different muscle groups in the body to reduce physical tension and stress.

- **Guided Imagery**: Using guided imagery, individuals can visualize calming scenes or experiences to relax the mind and body.
- **Yoga and Tai Chi**: These practices combine physical movement, breath control, and meditation to promote relaxation and emotional balance.

Fostering a positive outlook and practicing gratitude can significantly impact emotional maturity and regulation.

- **Gratitude Journaling**: Writing down things for which one is grateful can shift focus from negative to positive aspects of life.
- **Positive Affirmations**: Repeating positive affirmations can help reinforce a positive self-image and outlook.
- **Acts of Kindness**: Engaging in acts of kindness can boost mood and foster a sense of connection and empathy.

Sometimes, developing emotional regulation and maturity requires external support.

- **Therapy**: Seeking therapy from a mental health professional can provide individuals with tools and strategies to manage emotions effectively.
- **Support Groups**: Joining support groups can offer a sense of community and shared understanding, which can be beneficial in navigating emotional challenges.
- **Mindfulness or Emotional Intelligence Workshops**: Participating in workshops or courses focused on mindfulness or emotional intelligence can provide valuable

skills and insights.

Developing emotional regulation and emotional maturity is a journey that requires dedication and practice. By incorporating mindfulness, cognitive-behavioral techniques, emotional intelligence building, stress management, positivity practices, and seeking support, individuals can navigate life's ups and downs with greater ease and resilience. Remember, the key to emotional balance lies in self-awareness, self-compassion, and a willingness to grow and learn.

The Role of Self-Care in Emotional Balance

In the journey of life, emotional balance is like sailing a ship through ever-changing seas. It requires skill, awareness, and a deep understanding of oneself. Self-care plays a pivotal role in this journey, serving as both the anchor and the compass that guide us toward emotional equilibrium.

Self-care is the practice of taking an active role in protecting one's own well-being and happiness, particularly during periods of stress. It involves engaging in activities that nurture our physical, mental, and emotional health. Self-care is not a luxury; it's a necessity for maintaining emotional balance and overall well-being.

Emotional balance is the state of being able to manage our emotions in a way that is healthy and appropriate to the situation. It's about experiencing a full range of emotions without letting any one emotion dominate our lives. Self-care supports emotional balance by providing the tools and practices needed to manage stress, regulate emotions, and cultivate a positive mindset.

Self-Care Practices for Emotional Balance

1. **Physical Self-Care**: Taking care of our physical health is crucial for emotional balance. This includes regular exercise, a balanced diet, adequate sleep, and relaxation techniques such as deep breathing or yoga.
2. **Mental Self-Care**: Engaging in activities that stimulate and nourish the mind can help maintain emotional balance. This might involve reading, learning a new skill, practicing mindfulness, or seeking therapy when needed.
3. **Emotional Self-Care**: Cultivating emotional resilience is essential for emotional balance. This can be achieved through practices such as journaling, expressing gratitude, setting boundaries, and engaging in activities that bring joy and fulfillment.
4. **Social Self-Care**: Building and maintaining healthy relationships is a key aspect of self-care. It's important to seek support from friends, family, or support groups, and to engage in social activities that foster connection and a sense of belonging.

Emotional regulation is the ability to manage and respond to our emotions in a healthy way. Self-care directly impacts our capacity for emotional regulation by providing the tools and practices needed to manage stress, cultivate mindfulness, and build resilience. By prioritizing self-care, we can navigate life's challenges with greater ease and emotional stability.

Despite its importance, many people face barriers to practicing self-care, such as time constraints, guilt, or a lack of awareness. Overcoming these barriers requires intentionality and self-compassion. It's important to recognize that self-care is not selfish; it's essential for our well-being and our ability to care for others.

Integrating self-care into daily life involves making it a priority and establishing routines that support our well-being. This might include setting aside time each day for self-care activities, creating a self-care plan, and being mindful of the need for balance and flexibility in our self-care practices.

The role of self-care in emotional balance cannot be overstated. It is the foundation upon which we build our emotional resilience and navigate the complexities of life. By prioritizing self-care, we can cultivate a sense of inner peace and stability, enabling us to face life's challenges with grace and strength.

Navigating Life's Challenges with Resilience

Resilience is the beacon that guides us through the storms of life, enabling us to bounce back from adversity and maintain balance amidst life's challenges. It's the inner strength that helps us navigate rough seas and emerge stronger on the other side. In this part of the chapter, we'll explore strategies for building resilience, drawing upon the wisdom of those who have weathered life's storms and emerged with a deeper sense of purpose and strength.

One of the cornerstones of resilience is a strong support network. Having people we can rely on, who offer understanding, encouragement, and a listening ear, can make all the difference when we're facing tough times. Cultivating meaningful relationships with family, friends, and community members provides a safety net that can catch us when we fall and help us rise again.

A positive outlook is a powerful tool for building resilience. It's about seeing the glass as half full, finding the silver lining in every cloud, and maintaining hope even in the darkest of times. Cultivating a positive outlook involves practicing gratitude, focusing on what we can control, and embracing a growth mindset that sees challenges as opportunities for learning and growth.

Our past experiences, both good and bad, are a rich source of wisdom and strength. By reflecting on how we've navigated previous challenges, we can gain insights into our coping mechanisms, strengths, and areas for growth. Learning from our past helps us build resilience by showing us that we have faced adversity before and emerged stronger.

Self-compassion is a key component of resilience. It involves treating ourselves with the same kindness and understanding that we would offer a good friend. When we're going through tough times, being gentle with ourselves, acknowledging our pain, and giving ourselves permission to heal can help us bounce back more quickly and maintain emotional balance.

Resilient individuals set realistic goals and take action to achieve them. This proactive approach helps build a sense of purpose and control, which are important for resilience. By breaking down our goals into manageable steps and celebrating our progress, we can maintain momentum and stay focused on moving forward.

Mindfulness and stress reduction techniques, such as meditation, deep breathing, and yoga, can help us stay centered and calm in the face of life's challenges. These practices help us stay present in the moment, reduce anxiety and stress, and cultivate a sense of inner peace that supports resilience.

Sometimes, building resilience requires seeking professional help. Therapists, counselors, and mental health professionals can provide guidance, support, and strategies for navigating life's challenges and building resilience. There's no shame in seeking help; it's a sign of strength and a step toward greater well-being.

Navigating life's challenges with resilience is a journey of self-discovery, growth, and empowerment. By developing a strong support network, cultivating a positive outlook, learning from past experiences, embracing self-compassion, setting realistic goals, practicing mindfulness, and seeking professional help when needed, we can build the resilience needed to weather life's storms and emerge stronger and more balanced.

Integrating Emotional Regulation into Daily Life

Emotional regulation is a vital skill that helps us navigate the ebbs and flows of life with grace and resilience. Integrating emotional regulation into daily life is about more than just managing our emotions; it's about cultivating a deep sense of inner peace and well-being. In this final section, we'll explore practical tips and examples for applying emotional regulation techniques in common scenarios, such as managing stress at work, dealing with relationship conflicts, and coping with unexpected setbacks.

The workplace can be a significant source of stress, but emotional regulation can help us stay calm and focused. When faced with a tight deadline or a challenging project, take a moment to practice deep breathing or mindfulness to center yourself. Remind yourself that you have the skills and resources to handle the task at hand. Break down the project into manageable steps and tackle them one at a time, celebrating small victories along the way.

Relationship conflicts are inevitable, but emotional regulation can help us navigate them with compassion and understanding. When a disagreement arises, take a step back and assess your emotions. Are you feeling angry, hurt, or frustrated? Acknowledge these feelings without judgment. Then, communicate your emotions and needs clearly and calmly, without blaming or criticizing the other person. Listen actively to their perspective and work together to find a solution that meets both of your needs.

Life is full of surprises, and not all of them are pleasant. When faced with an unexpected setback, such as a job loss or a health issue, it's natural to feel a range of emotions. Allow yourself to feel these emotions without getting overwhelmed by them. Seek support from friends, family, or a mental health professional. Focus on what you can control and take proactive steps to address the situation. Remember that setbacks are often temporary and can lead to new opportunities and growth.

Cultivating a sense of gratitude and positivity is a powerful way to enhance emotional regulation. Start each day by reflecting on things you're grateful for, no matter how small. Throughout the day, try to focus on the positive aspects of your experiences, even in challenging situations. This shift in perspective can help reduce stress and increase emotional well-being.

Setting healthy boundaries is crucial for emotional regulation. It's important to recognize your limits and communicate them clearly to others. Make self-care a priority, and ensure that you're taking time to relax, recharge, and engage in activities that bring you joy. By taking care of yourself, you'll be better equipped to handle life's challenges with emotional balance and resilience.

Integrating emotional regulation into daily life is a journey that requires practice, patience, and self-compassion. By applying these techniques in everyday scenarios, we can navigate life's challenges with greater ease and maintain a sense of emotional balance and well-being.

References

- Gross, J. J. (2015). *Emotion Regulation: Conceptual and Practical Issues*. In T. A. R. Schnitker & R. A. Emmons (Eds.), *Handbook of Positive Psychology*. Oxford University Press.
- Mayer, J. D., & Salovey, P. (1997). *What is Emotional Intelligence?* In P. Salovey & D. J. Sluyter (Eds.), *Emotional Development and Emotional Intelligence: Educational Implications*. Basic Books.
- Goleman, D. (1995). *Emotional Intelligence*. Bantam Books.
- Kabat-Zinn, J. (1994). *Wherever You Go, There You Are: Mindfulness Meditation in Everyday Life*. Hyperion.
- Linehan, M. M. (1993). *Cognitive-Behavioral Treatment of Borderline Personality Disorder*. Guilford Press.
- Neff, K. D. (2011). *Self-Compassion: The Proven Power of Being Kind to Yourself*. William Morrow.
- Shapiro, S. L., & Carlson, L. E. (2009). *The Art and Science of Mindfulness: Integrating Mindfulness into Psychology and the Helping Professions*. American Psychological Association.
- Southwick, S. M., & Charney, D. S. (2012). *Resilience: The Science of Mastering Life's Greatest Challenges*. Cambridge University Press.
- Fredrickson, B. L. (2009). *Positivity: Top-Notch Research Reveals the 3 to 1 Ratio That Will Change Your Life*. Three Rivers Press.

****

Chapter 7

Steering Through Social Storms:

Managing Relationships and Expectations

In the chapter titled "Steering Through Social Storms: Managing Relationships and Expectations," it's important to address the complexities of interpersonal relationships and social media and their impact on stress. Here are three to five key points or subheadings that should be included in this chapter:

In today's interconnected world, relationships and social media play a significant role in shaping our stress levels. The double-edged sword of connectivity means that while social networks can offer support and a sense of belonging, they can also be sources of conflict, comparison, and information overload, contributing to stress and mental health challenges.

Relationships, whether personal or professional, can be both a source of comfort and a cause of stress. Supportive relationships provide a sense of connection and security, helping to buffer against life's challenges. However, conflicts, misunderstandings, and unmet expectations within relationships can lead to increased stress and emotional turmoil.

Social media, on the other hand, has transformed the way we connect and communicate. It offers opportunities for staying in touch with loved ones, networking, and sharing experiences. However, the constant connectivity can also lead to stress. The pressure to maintain an idealized online persona, the exposure to curated highlights of others' lives, and the bombardment of information can lead to feelings of inadequacy, comparison, and fear of missing out (FOMO).

Social media's impact on mental health is complex. On one hand, it can provide valuable social connections and support, especially for those who may feel isolated in their offline lives. On the other hand, excessive use of social media has been linked to increased risks of depression, anxiety, loneliness, self-harm, and even suicidal thoughts.

The negative aspects of social media often stem from how it's used and the content consumed. Inadequacy about one's life or appearance, fear of missing out, isolation, depression, anxiety, cyberbullying, and self-absorption are some of the challenges associated with social media use. It's crucial to be mindful of these potential pitfalls and strive for a balanced approach to social media consumption.

In the digital age, managing stress has become increasingly complex, with the constant connectivity and bombardment of information contributing to heightened anxiety and mental health challenges. To navigate these "social storms," it's essential to adopt strategies that promote balance and well-being.

One of the key strategies for managing stress in the digital age is setting boundaries around social media and technology use. Excessive screen time and constant notifications can lead to information overload, exacerbating stress and anxiety. By limiting time on social media, turning off notifications, and setting specific times for checking devices, individuals can reduce interruptions and create a sense of control over their digital lives. Establishing these boundaries helps mitigate the fear of missing out (FOMO) and the pressure to be constantly available, allowing for more focused and meaningful engagement with the online world.

In an era where digital interactions often replace face-to-face communication, cultivating meaningful connections has become crucial for emotional well-being. Prioritizing quality over quantity in social interactions can lead to more fulfilling relationships that provide support and positivity. Engaging in deep, authentic conversations and nurturing connections with friends, family, and community members can counteract feelings of loneliness and isolation often exacerbated by superficial online interactions. By focusing on building strong, supportive relationships, individuals can create a social network that serves as a buffer against stress and enhances overall life satisfaction.

Self-care is an essential component of managing stress in the digital age. Engaging in activities that promote relaxation and well-being, such as exercise, meditation, and hobbies, can help individuals recharge and maintain emotional balance. Regular physical activity has been shown to reduce stress, anxiety, and depression, while mindfulness practices like meditation can enhance emotional regulation and resilience. Finding joy in hobbies and creative pursuits can provide a sense of accomplishment and distraction from stressors. Prioritizing self-care helps address fear points related to burnout and emotional exhaustion, fostering a sense of inner peace and contentment.

In the digital age, the impact of social media and technology on mental health has become a growing concern. With the constant barrage of information, the pressure to maintain an online presence, and the comparison trap that social media can create, it's no surprise that many individuals are experiencing increased levels of stress and mental health issues. Seeking professional help can be a crucial step in addressing these challenges and finding a path toward emotional well-being.

Mental health professionals are equipped with the knowledge and tools to help individuals navigate the complexities of stress and mental health issues in the digital age. They can provide a safe and confidential space to explore the impact of technology on one's life and offer personalized strategies for managing stress and improving mental health.

1. **Tailored Coping Strategies**: Therapists can help individuals

develop coping strategies that are tailored to their specific needs and challenges. This might include techniques for managing anxiety triggered by social media, strategies for setting boundaries around technology use, or methods for cultivating a more positive online experience.

2. **Support and Validation**: Professional help offers a supportive and validating environment where individuals can express their feelings and concerns without judgment. This can be particularly valuable in a world where online interactions can sometimes feel superficial or invalidating.

3. **Exploring Underlying Issues**: Therapy can provide an opportunity to explore underlying issues that may be contributing to stress or mental health problems. This could include examining patterns of negative self-talk, addressing past traumas, or exploring issues related to self-esteem and identity.

There are various modalities of professional help available to address the challenges of the digital age, each with its own advantages:

1. **Traditional Therapy**: In-person therapy sessions offer a face-to-face connection with a mental health professional. This can be particularly beneficial for individuals who value the personal interaction and find it easier to communicate in a physical space.

2. **Online Counseling**: Online counseling platforms provide access to therapy from the comfort of one's home. This can be a convenient option for those with busy schedules, limited mobility, or a preference for digital communication.

3. **Support Groups**: Support groups, whether in-person or online, offer a sense of community and shared experience. They can be a valuable resource for individuals seeking connection with others who understand their struggles.

Seeking professional help can address several fear points associated with the digital age:

1. **Fear of Isolation**: Therapy and support groups can provide a sense of connection and community, counteracting feelings of isolation that can arise from excessive technology use.
2. **Fear of Losing Control**: Professional help can empower individuals to regain control over their digital lives by setting boundaries and developing healthy habits.
3. **Fear of Judgment**: The confidential and non-judgmental nature of therapy provides a safe space for individuals to express their concerns without fear of judgment.

Seeking professional help is a vital component of managing stress and mental health issues in the digital age. By providing tailored coping strategies, support, and a deeper understanding of underlying issues, mental health professionals can guide individuals toward a more balanced and fulfilling life in an increasingly digital world.

Setting healthy boundaries in relationships is crucial for maintaining emotional well-being and fostering respectful, fulfilling interactions. Whether with friends, family, or colleagues, establishing clear boundaries helps prevent feelings of resentment, burnout, and emotional exhaustion. This comprehensive exploration delves into the importance of identifying personal limits and communicating boundaries effectively.

Recognizing one's own limits in relationships is the foundation of setting healthy boundaries. It involves self-awareness and understanding what is emotionally draining versus what is nurturing. Personal limits vary from person to person and can change over time. They might include the amount of time and energy one is willing to invest in a relationship, the types of behavior one finds acceptable, and the need for personal space and privacy.

To identify personal limits, individuals can reflect on past experiences in relationships and note situations that led to feelings of discomfort, resentment, or exhaustion. It's important to listen to one's own feelings and needs, as they are key indicators of where boundaries should be set.

Once personal limits are identified, the next step is effectively communicating these boundaries to others. This can be challenging, especially in relationships where boundaries have been blurred or nonexistent. However, clear and assertive communication is essential for establishing and maintaining healthy boundaries.

- **Be Clear and Specific**: Clearly state what is acceptable and what is not. Use specific language to avoid misunderstandings. For example, instead of saying, "I need space," say, "I need an hour of alone time each evening to unwind."
- **Use "I" Statements**: Frame your boundaries in terms of your own needs and feelings rather than blaming or accusing the other person. For example, "I feel overwhelmed when I have too many social commitments. I need to limit my outings to two per week."
- **Be Assertive but Respectful**: Assertiveness is about expressing your needs confidently and respectfully. It's not about being aggressive or confrontational. Maintain a calm and respectful tone when communicating your boundaries.
- **Practice and Prepare**: If you anticipate resistance or discomfort, practice what you want to say beforehand. You can even role-play with a trusted friend or therapist to build confidence.

Setting boundaries often involves navigating pushback from those who may be used to the status quo. It's important to stay firm and consistent in enforcing your boundaries, even when faced with resistance. Reiterate your needs calmly and assertively, and avoid getting drawn into arguments or justifications. Remember, setting boundaries is about honoring your own well-being, not about pleasing others.

Setting healthy boundaries can address several fear points in relationships:

- **Fear of Conflict**: Clear communication of boundaries can reduce the likelihood of misunderstandings and conflicts.
- **Fear of Losing Relationships**: While some relationships may change or even end when boundaries are set, those that remain are likely to be healthier and more respectful.
- **Fear of Being Selfish**: Setting boundaries is not selfish; it's a form of self-care. It allows you to maintain your well-being so that you can engage in relationships more fully and authentically.

Setting healthy boundaries in relationships is an essential skill for emotional well-being. It involves identifying personal limits, communicating them effectively, and navigating any pushback with assertiveness and respect. By setting boundaries, individuals can build more fulfilling and respectful relationships that honor their needs and values.

Navigating Social Media Mindfully

Navigating social media mindfully is essential in today's digital age, where online platforms have become integral to our daily lives. The constant influx of information and the pressure to stay connected can lead to stress, anxiety, and a sense of overwhelm. By adopting a mindful approach to social media, we can enjoy its benefits while minimizing its negative impact on our mental health and well-being.

A digital detox involves taking intentional breaks from social media and other digital devices to disconnect and recharge. This can be a set period, such as a weekend or a specific time each day when you unplug from all digital devices. The aim is to reduce dependence on social media, create space for offline activities, and prevent digital overload.

Mindful usage of social media involves being intentional and present with your online activities. It means being aware of why you're using social media, how much time you're spending on it, and the quality of your interactions. Here are some tips for practicing mindful social media usage:

- **Set time limits**: Use built-in app features or external tools to set daily time limits for social media usage. This can help prevent excessive scrolling and ensure you have time for other important activities.
- **Be intentional**: Before opening a social media app, ask yourself why you're doing it. Are you looking for connection, entertainment, or information? Being clear about your purpose can help you use social media more mindfully.
- **Focus on quality interactions**: Engage in meaningful conversations and interactions that add value to your life. Avoid mindless scrolling and instead, comment on posts, share content that resonates with you, and connect with others in a thoughtful way.

The content we consume on social media can significantly impact our mood and overall well-being. Curating a positive online experience involves actively managing your social media feed to ensure it aligns with your values and promotes positivity. Here are some tips for creating a more uplifting social media environment:

- **Follow inspiring accounts**: Seek out accounts that inspire, motivate, and uplift you. This could be public figures, organizations, or friends who share positive content.
- **Use filters and unfollow negative content**: Most social media platforms have features that allow you to hide or unfollow content that doesn't serve you. Don't hesitate to use these tools to filter out negativity and customize your feed.
- **Engage in positive communities**: Join online groups or communities that share your interests and values. These spaces can offer support, inspiration, and a sense of belonging.

Mindful social media usage can help address common fear points associated with digital interactions:

- **Fear of missing out (FOMO)**: By setting boundaries and being intentional with your social media use, you can reduce the anxiety associated with FOMO and focus on enjoying your present experiences.
- **Fear of negative comparison**: Curating your feed to include positive and inspiring content can help mitigate the tendency to compare yourself unfavorably to others.
- **Fear of disconnection**: By prioritizing quality interactions and engaging in positive online communities, you can foster a sense of connection and belonging.

Navigating social media mindfully is about finding a balance that allows you to enjoy the benefits of digital connectivity without sacrificing your mental health and well-being. By practicing digital detox, mindful usage, and curating a positive online experience, you can create a healthier relationship with social media that enriches your life rather than detracts from it.

Balancing Expectations in Relationships

Balancing expectations in relationships is a delicate art that requires communication, understanding, and self-awareness. Expectations, whether spoken or unspoken, play a significant role in the dynamics of any relationship. When managed well, they can lead to fulfilling and harmonious connections. However, unrealistic or uncommunicated expectations can lead to stress, disappointment, and conflict.

Expectations in relationships can range from how we anticipate being treated to what we assume our roles and responsibilities should be. They are often shaped by our past experiences, cultural norms, and personal beliefs. Managing these expectations is crucial for maintaining a healthy and stress-free relationship.

- **Open Communication**: The foundation of managing expectations is open and honest communication. It's important to express your needs and desires clearly and listen to your partner's as well. Regular check-ins can help ensure that both parties are on the same page and prevent misunderstandings.
- **Flexibility**: Being flexible and adaptable is key to managing expectations. Life is unpredictable, and being able to adjust your expectations in response to changing circumstances can reduce stress and prevent resentment.
- **Realistic Goal-Setting**: Setting realistic and achievable goals for your relationship can help manage expectations. It's

important to recognize that no relationship is perfect and that challenges are a normal part of any partnership.

Self-compassion and forgiveness are vital components of balancing expectations in relationships. They allow us to navigate the inevitable disappointments and misunderstandings with grace and resilience.

- **Self-Compassion**: Practicing self-compassion means treating yourself with the same kindness and understanding that you would offer a friend. It involves acknowledging that it's okay to have limitations and make mistakes. When you're compassionate with yourself, you're more likely to manage your expectations realistically and handle relationship stress more effectively.
- **Forgiveness**: Forgiveness is a powerful tool for managing relationship stress. It involves letting go of resentment and anger towards yourself or your partner for not meeting certain expectations. Forgiveness doesn't mean condoning hurtful behavior, but it does mean choosing to move forward with understanding and empathy.

Balancing expectations in relationships can directly impact common fear points:

- **Fear of Rejection**: By communicating openly and setting realistic expectations, individuals can reduce the fear of rejection, as both partners have a clear understanding of each other's needs and boundaries.
- **Fear of Conflict**: Practicing flexibility and forgiveness can help mitigate the fear of conflict, as it fosters a more accepting and understanding relationship dynamic.
- **Fear of Not Being Good Enough**: Self-compassion

addresses the fear of not being good enough by promoting self-acceptance and recognizing that imperfection is a natural part of being human.

Balancing expectations in relationships is essential for fostering a healthy and fulfilling connection. By managing expectations through open communication, flexibility, and realistic goal-setting, and by practicing self-compassion and forgiveness, individuals can navigate relationship stress more effectively and build stronger, more resilient partnerships.

References

- Townsend, J. S., & Cloud, H. (1992). *Boundaries: When to Say Yes, How to Say No to Take Control of Your Life.* Zondervan.
- Lancer, D. (2017). *Codependency for Dummies.* John Wiley & Sons.*
- Tawwab, N. (2021). *Set Boundaries, Find Peace: A Guide to Reclaiming Yourself.* TarcherPerigee References
- American Psychological Association. (2020). *Stress in America™ 2020: A National Mental Health Crisis.* https://www.apa.org/news/press/releases/stress/2020/report-october
- Twenge, J. M., & Campbell, W. K. (2018). *The associations between screen time and mental health in young adults: Evidence from three large datasets.* Psychiatric Quarterly, 89(3), 531-546. https://doi.org/10.1007/s11126-018-9598-1
- Vannucci, A., Flannery, K. M., & McCauley Ohannessian, C. (2017). *Social media use and anxiety in emerging adults.*

Journal of Affective Disorders, 207, 163-166.
https://doi.org/10.1016/j.jad.2016.08.040.

- Newport, C. (2019). *Digital Minimalism: Choosing a Focused Life in a Noisy World*. Portfolio/Penguin.
- Kabat-Zinn, J. (1994). *Wherever You Go, There You Are: Mindfulness Meditation in Everyday Life*. Hyperion.
- Kross, E. (2021). *Chatter: The Voice in Our Head, Why It Matters, and How to Harness It*. Crown.
- Gottman, J. M., & Silver, N. (1999). *The Seven Principles for Making Marriage Work*. Crown Publishing Group.
- Neff, K. D. (2011). *Self-Compassion: The Proven Power of Being Kind to Yourself*. William Morrow.
- Luskin, F. (2002). *Forgive for Good: A Proven Prescription for Health and Happiness*. HarperOne.

****

Chapter 8

Fortifying Your Vessel:

Building Resilience Against Life's Challenges

In the chapter titled "Fortifying Your Vessel: Building Resilience Against Life's Challenges," we embark on a journey to explore the essence of resilience and the strategies that can help us strengthen our mental and emotional fortitude. This chapter is a guide to navigating the tumultuous seas of life with grace and strength, ensuring that we can withstand the storms that come our way.

Resilience is the anchor that keeps our ship steady in the face of adversity. It is the ability to bounce back from stress, challenges, and setbacks, and to emerge stronger and wiser. Resilience is not about avoiding difficulties but about facing them head-on and learning from them. It is a crucial trait for maintaining mental and emotional well-being, as it enables us to navigate life's ups and downs with confidence and equanimity.

At the heart of resilience lies emotional resilience—the capacity to manage our emotions and responses to stress. Self-awareness plays a pivotal role in this process, as it allows us to recognize our emotional triggers and patterns. By developing strategies for emotional regulation, such as mindfulness, deep breathing, and cognitive restructuring, we can cultivate a sense of inner calm and balance, even in the midst of turmoil.

Mental resilience is the sail that propels us forward, powered by the winds of positive thinking and optimism. It involves cultivating a mindset that focuses on solutions and opportunities rather than dwelling on problems and obstacles. Effective problem-solving skills, such as breaking down challenges into manageable parts and approaching them with creativity, are essential for navigating the complexities of life.

No ship can sail without a crew, and social resilience is about building and nurturing the supportive relationships that form our crew. These connections provide comfort, encouragement, and a sense of belonging, which are vital for weathering life's storms. Seeking help from friends, family, or professionals when needed is a sign of strength, as it shows a willingness to reach out and lean on others for support.

Resilience is a skill that can be practiced and honed every day. Setting realistic goals and celebrating progress, however small, builds confidence and a sense of achievement. Adapting to change and embracing a growth mindset are key to remaining flexible and open to new possibilities. By incorporating these practices into our daily lives, we can fortify our vessels and set sail towards a future filled with resilience and hope.

In conclusion, "Fortifying Your Vessel: Building Resilience Against Life's Challenges" is a chapter dedicated to empowering readers with the tools and insights needed to strengthen their mental and emotional resilience. By understanding and embracing the principles of resilience, we can prepare ourselves to face future stresses with greater confidence and equanimity, ensuring that we remain steadfast and strong, no matter what life throws our way.

Understanding Resilience

Resilience is a term that has gained significant attention in the realms of psychology, personal development, and leadership. It is often described as the ability to bounce back from adversity, stress, and challenges. But resilience is more than just a buzzword; it is a fundamental quality that enables individuals to navigate life's ups and downs with grace and strength.

At its core, resilience is the capacity to recover quickly from difficulties. It is the mental, emotional, and sometimes physical fortitude that allows us to face setbacks, adapt to change, and keep moving forward. Resilience is not about avoiding problems or living a life free from pain. Instead, it is about embracing challenges, learning from them, and emerging stronger.

Resilience is often likened to a muscle that can be strengthened over time. Just as physical exercise builds physical strength, facing and overcoming obstacles can build resilience. It involves a combination of skills, attitudes, and behaviors that can be developed and honed through life experiences.

Resilience is crucial for several reasons. First and foremost, it is a key factor in maintaining mental and emotional well-being. Life is inherently unpredictable, and stress is an inevitable part of the human experience. Resilience equips us with the tools to manage stress effectively, preventing it from overwhelming us and leading to burnout or mental health issues.

Furthermore, resilience is essential for personal growth and development. It encourages a mindset of learning and growth, where challenges are seen as opportunities for self-discovery and improvement. This mindset fosters a sense of purpose and direction, even in the face of adversity.

In today's fast-paced and ever-changing world, resilience is also a critical skill for success. Whether in personal or professional contexts, the ability to adapt to change, overcome obstacles, and persevere in the pursuit of goals is invaluable. Resilient individuals are more likely to achieve their objectives and find fulfillment in their endeavors.

While some people may naturally possess a higher level of resilience, it is a quality that can be cultivated and strengthened over time. Here are some strategies for building resilience:

- **Foster Positive Relationships**: Surrounding yourself with supportive friends, family, and colleagues can provide a strong social network that offers encouragement and assistance during tough times.
- **Develop a Growth Mindset**: Embrace challenges as opportunities for learning and growth. Focus on the lessons that can be gleaned from setbacks rather than dwelling on the negatives.
- **Practice Self-Care**: Taking care of your physical, emotional, and mental health is crucial for resilience. Regular exercise, adequate sleep, healthy eating, and mindfulness practices can all contribute to a strong foundation of well-being.
- **Set Realistic Goals**: Having clear and achievable goals provides a sense of purpose and direction. Break down larger goals into smaller, manageable steps and celebrate your progress along the way.
- **Cultivate Optimism**: Maintaining a positive outlook, even in the face of adversity, can help you stay motivated and focused. Practice gratitude and look for the silver linings in difficult situations.

Understanding resilience is the first step in cultivating this vital quality. By recognizing the importance of resilience and actively working to strengthen it, individuals can navigate life's challenges with greater ease and confidence. Resilience is not just about surviving; it's about thriving in the face of adversity.

Building Emotional Resilience

In a world that often feels like a tempest of emotions, building emotional resilience is akin to constructing a sturdy ship that can navigate through the stormiest of seas. Emotional resilience is the ability to adapt to and recover from emotional challenges, stress, and adversity. It's about developing a core of inner strength that allows you to maintain your equilibrium and thrive, even in the face of life's inevitable ups and downs.

Self-awareness is the foundation of emotional resilience. It's the compass that guides you through the turbulent waters of your emotions, helping you recognize your emotional triggers and manage your responses. By developing self-awareness, you become attuned to your feelings, thoughts, and behaviors, allowing you to understand why you react the way you do in certain situations.

- **Identifying Emotional Triggers**: Start by identifying the situations, people, or thoughts that trigger strong emotional responses in you. These triggers can be external, such as a stressful work environment, or internal, such as negative self-talk.
- **Reflecting on Emotions**: Take time to reflect on your emotions. Ask yourself what you're feeling, why you're feeling it, and how it's affecting your behavior. This reflection can provide valuable insights into your emotional patterns and help you develop healthier coping mechanisms.

Emotional regulation is the skill of managing and modulating your emotional reactions in a healthy way. It's about steering your ship through stormy emotions, so you don't get swept away by the waves of anger, anxiety, or sadness.

- **Mindfulness**: Mindfulness is a powerful tool for emotional regulation. It involves staying present and fully engaged in the moment without judgment. By practicing mindfulness, you can observe your emotions without getting caught up in them, creating space to choose how you respond.
- **Deep Breathing**: Deep breathing is a simple yet effective technique for calming the nervous system and reducing emotional intensity. When you feel overwhelmed by emotions, take a few deep breaths, focusing on the sensation of the air filling your lungs and then slowly exhaling.
- **Cognitive Restructuring**: Cognitive restructuring is a cognitive-behavioral therapy technique that involves challenging and changing negative thought patterns. By reframing your thoughts in a more positive or realistic light, you can alter your emotional responses and reduce stress.

Building emotional resilience is an ongoing process that requires nurturing and practice. Here are some additional strategies to strengthen your emotional resilience:

- **Practice Self-Compassion**: Treat yourself with kindness and understanding, especially during tough times. Self-compassion can help you navigate emotional challenges with greater ease and resilience.
- **Develop a Support Network**: Surround yourself with supportive friends and family who can provide encouragement and perspective when you're facing emotional

difficulties.

- **Cultivate a Positive Outlook**: Focus on the positive aspects of your life and practice gratitude. A positive outlook can bolster your emotional resilience and help you see challenges as opportunities for growth.

Building emotional resilience is a journey that empowers you to face life's challenges with courage and grace. By developing self-awareness, practicing emotional regulation, and nurturing your inner strength, you can fortify your vessel and sail confidently through the ever-changing seas of life.

Strengthening Mental Resilience

In the journey of life, mental resilience is the inner strength that empowers us to navigate challenges, adapt to change, and emerge stronger from adversity. It's the mental fortitude that enables us to maintain our balance amidst the storms of life. This section explores the vital role of positive thinking and problem-solving skills in building and strengthening mental resilience.

Positive thinking is a cornerstone of mental resilience. It's not about ignoring life's difficulties or pretending everything is perfect. Instead, it's about approaching challenges with a mindset of optimism and hope. Positive thinking involves focusing on the good, looking for solutions, and believing in one's ability to overcome obstacles.

- **Cultivating Optimism**: Optimism is the belief that good things will happen and that challenges can be overcome. It's a perspective that can be cultivated by practicing gratitude, visualizing positive outcomes, and reframing negative thoughts.

- **The Benefits of Positive Thinking**: Research has shown that positive thinking can reduce stress, improve physical health, and enhance psychological well-being. It's associated with greater resilience, better coping skills, and a lower risk of depression and anxiety.

Effective problem-solving is a critical component of mental resilience. It's the ability to identify problems, generate solutions, and implement them effectively. Problem-solving skills enable us to break down challenges into manageable parts and find creative solutions.

- **Breaking Down Problems**: When faced with a complex problem, it's helpful to break it down into smaller, more manageable parts. This makes it easier to understand the issue and identify potential solutions.
- **Seeking Creative Solutions**: Creativity is a valuable asset in problem-solving. It involves thinking outside the box, exploring different perspectives, and being open to innovative ideas.
- **Implementing Solutions**: Once a solution has been identified, the next step is to put it into action. This requires planning, persistence, and adaptability.

Strengthening mental resilience has a profound impact on our lives. It enables us to:

- **Handle Stress More Effectively**: Resilient individuals are better equipped to manage stress and bounce back from setbacks.
- **Adapt to Change**: In a world that's constantly changing, mental resilience helps us adapt to new situations and embrace change as an opportunity for growth.

- **Achieve Personal and Professional Goals**: Mental resilience provides the inner strength needed to pursue goals, overcome obstacles, and realize our potential.

Strengthening mental resilience is a journey that requires commitment and practice. By cultivating positive thinking and honing our problem-solving skills, we can build a strong foundation of resilience that will support us through life's challenges. It's a process of growth and empowerment that leads to a more fulfilling and resilient life.

Cultivating Social Resilience

In the tapestry of life, social resilience is the thread that weaves together supportive relationships and connections, forming a fabric that can withstand the wear and tear of life's challenges. Cultivating social resilience is about nurturing these bonds and understanding the vital role they play in our ability to bounce back from adversity.

The importance of building support networks cannot be overstated. These networks consist of friends, family, colleagues, and community members who provide emotional support, practical assistance, and a sense of belonging. Strong social connections are associated with numerous benefits, including improved mental health, increased happiness, and a longer life span.

- **Nurturing Relationships**: Invest time and energy in nurturing relationships that are positive and supportive. This might involve regular check-ins, spending quality time together, and showing appreciation for one another.
- **Diversifying Social Connections**: A diverse social network can provide a range of perspectives and support. This might include close friends and family, as well as acquaintances and

members of community groups or clubs.

- **Building Community**: Engaging in community activities or volunteering can foster a sense of belonging and contribute to a support network that extends beyond personal relationships.

There are times when the challenges we face are too difficult to manage alone, and seeking help is a sign of strength, not weakness. Whether it's reaching out to a trusted friend or consulting a professional, asking for assistance is a crucial aspect of social resilience.

- **Recognizing the Need for Help**: Pay attention to signs that you might need support, such as feeling overwhelmed, experiencing persistent sadness or anxiety, or struggling to cope with daily tasks.
- **Reaching Out to Friends and Family**: Sometimes, simply talking to someone you trust can provide relief and a new perspective on a problem. Don't hesitate to reach out to friends or family members when you need support.
- **Consulting Professionals**: If you're facing challenges that are impacting your mental health or well-being, consider seeking help from a mental health professional, counselor, or therapist. They can provide specialized support and guidance to help you navigate difficult times.

Cultivating social resilience has a profound impact on our overall resilience. It provides a safety net that can catch us when we fall and a cheering section to celebrate our victories. Social support can buffer against the negative effects of stress, reduce the risk of mental health issues, and enhance our ability to cope with life's challenges.

- **Reducing Isolation and Loneliness**: Strong social

connections can mitigate feelings of isolation and loneliness, which are significant risk factors for mental health problems.

- **Enhancing Coping Skills**: Support from others can provide new coping strategies, emotional comfort, and practical assistance in times of need.
- **Fostering a Sense of Belonging**: Feeling part of a community or group can provide a sense of identity and purpose, contributing to our overall sense of well-being.

Cultivating social resilience is about recognizing the power of connection and the importance of seeking and offering support. By building support networks and reaching out for help when needed, we can create a strong foundation of social resilience that empowers us to face life's challenges with confidence and grace.

Practicing Resilience in Daily Life

Resilience is not just a quality to be admired from afar; it's a skill to be practiced and cultivated in our daily lives. Like a garden that needs tending, our resilience requires attention, care, and consistent effort to flourish. This section explores how setting realistic goals and adapting to change are integral to practicing resilience in our everyday lives.

Goals give our lives direction and purpose, but the key to building resilience lies in setting goals that are realistic and achievable. When we set goals that are too lofty or vague, we set ourselves up for disappointment and frustration. On the other hand, attainable goals provide a sense of accomplishment and progress, which are vital for nurturing our resilience.

- **SMART Goals**: Embrace the concept of SMART goals—Specific, Measurable, Achievable, Relevant, and

Time-bound. This framework helps ensure that your goals are well-defined and attainable within a reasonable timeframe.

- **Break It Down**: Large goals can be overwhelming. Break them down into smaller, manageable tasks. Each small victory builds confidence and reinforces your belief in your ability to overcome challenges.
- **Celebrate Progress**: Recognize and celebrate your progress, no matter how small. Acknowledging your achievements reinforces positive emotions and motivates you to continue striving toward your goals.

Change is an inevitable part of life, and our ability to adapt to it is a cornerstone of resilience. Embracing change, rather than resisting it, allows us to grow and learn from new experiences.

- **Stay Flexible**: Cultivate flexibility by keeping an open mind and being willing to adjust your plans as needed. Flexibility enables you to navigate unexpected changes without losing your sense of direction.
- **Maintain a Growth Mindset**: A growth mindset, as opposed to a fixed mindset, embraces the belief that abilities and intelligence can be developed through effort and learning. This mindset encourages you to see change as an opportunity for growth rather than a threat.
- **Seek Support**: During times of change, lean on your support network for guidance and encouragement. Sharing your experiences and seeking advice can provide valuable perspectives and help you navigate transitions more smoothly.

Resilience can be practiced in various everyday scenarios, from handling work-related stress to dealing with personal setbacks. Here are some examples:

- **Workplace Challenges**: When faced with a difficult project or a tight deadline, break the task into smaller steps, focus on what you can control, and seek support from colleagues when needed.
- **Personal Setbacks**: In the face of personal setbacks, such as a failed relationship or a health issue, allow yourself to grieve, reflect on what you've learned, and focus on building a positive future.
- **Unexpected Changes**: When unexpected changes occur, such as a sudden job loss or a global pandemic, focus on adapting to the new reality, exploring new opportunities, and maintaining a hopeful outlook.

Practicing resilience in daily life is about setting realistic goals, embracing change, and applying these principles to the challenges we face. By doing so, we build a reservoir of strength and flexibility that enables us to navigate life's ups and downs with confidence and grace.

References

- Duckworth, A. (2016). *Grit: The Power of Passion and Perseverance*. Scribner.
- Southwick, S. M., & Charney, D. S. (2012). *Resilience: The Science of Mastering Life's Greatest Challenges*. Cambridge University Press.
- Cohen, S., & Wills, T. A. (1985). *Stress, social support, and the buffering hypothesis*. Psychological Bulletin, 98(2),

310-357.

- Uchino, B. N. (2009). *Understanding the links between social support and physical health: A life-span perspective with emphasis on the separability of perceived and received support.* Perspectives on Psychological Science, 4(3), 236-255.
- Seligman, M. E. P. (2002). *Authentic Happiness: Using the New Positive Psychology to Realize Your Potential for Lasting Fulfillment.* Free Press.
- Dweck, C. S. (2006). *Mindset: The New Psychology of Success.* Ballantine Books.
- Reivich, K., & Shatté, A. (2002). *The Resilience Factor: 7 Keys to Finding Your Inner Strength and Overcoming Life's Hurdles.* Broadway Books.
- Kabat-Zinn, J. (1994). *Wherever You Go, There You Are: Mindfulness Meditation in Everyday Life.* Hyperion.
- Neff, K. D. (2011). *Self-Compassion: The Proven Power of Being Kind to Yourself.* William Morrow.
- Gross, J. J. (2015). *Emotion Regulation: Conceptual and Practical Issues.* In T. A. R. Schnitker & R. A. Emmons (Eds.), *Handbook of Positive Psychology.* Oxford University Press.

****

Chapter 9

Guided by the Stars:

Setting Goals for Continued Growth

In the chapter titled "Guided by the Stars: Setting Goals for Continued Growth," we embark on a journey of self-discovery and personal development, aimed at guiding readers through the process of setting achievable goals for growth. This chapter is dedicated to those seeking to navigate the complexities of life with grace, managing stress, anxiety, negative thoughts, and finding balance amidst life's challenges.

The journey begins with the crucial step of self-reflection, a process that allows us to identify areas of personal growth. By looking inward, we can recognize patterns of overwhelming stress, anxiety, and negative self-talk that may be hindering our progress. This self-awareness is the first step towards transformation, providing the clarity needed to set specific, measurable goals that address our unique challenges.

With a clear understanding of our personal challenges, we move on to creating a roadmap for positive change. This involves developing a detailed plan to achieve our personal growth goals, breaking down larger objectives into smaller, manageable tasks. By setting realistic timelines and milestones, we can track our progress and maintain motivation, ensuring that each step taken is a step closer to our desired growth.

Central to our journey is the cultivation of mindfulness and emotional resilience. Mindfulness techniques, such as meditation and deep breathing, help us manage stress and anxiety, allowing us to maintain peace and calm in turbulent times. Emotional resilience, the ability to bounce back from adversity, is strengthened through exercises that build self-awareness and equip us to manage negative thoughts and toxic self-talk.

Achieving balance and harmony in daily life is essential for sustained growth. This requires creating a lifestyle that aligns with our personal values and priorities, setting boundaries to manage life's pressures effectively, and integrating self-care routines and relaxation techniques. By prioritizing balance, we can navigate life's challenges with greater ease and maintain a sense of well-being.

Finally, we acknowledge the importance of flexibility and adaptability in the goal-setting process. Life is dynamic, and circumstances can change unexpectedly. By being open to adjusting our goals in response to these changes, and celebrating our progress and learning from setbacks, we can ensure sustainable growth and continue on our path of self-improvement.

Identifying Personal Challenges and Growth Areas

In our journey through life, we often encounter challenges that test our resilience and strength. However, it's in the face of these challenges that we find opportunities for personal growth and transformation. Identifying personal challenges and growth areas is the first step toward a journey of self-improvement and empowerment. In this section, we will explore the importance of self-reflection, strategies for recognizing patterns of stress and negative self-talk, and tips for setting specific, measurable goals to overcome these challenges.

Self-reflection is a powerful tool for personal growth. It involves taking a step back to examine our thoughts, emotions, and behaviors, and to gain a deeper understanding of ourselves. Through self-reflection, we can identify areas in our lives that need attention and improvement. It allows us to recognize our strengths and weaknesses, and to understand how our past experiences have shaped us.

- **Embrace Vulnerability**: Allow yourself to be vulnerable during self-reflection. It's okay to acknowledge your fears, doubts, and insecurities. This honesty is the first step toward growth.
- **Practice Mindfulness**: Incorporate mindfulness into your self-reflection routine. Being present in the moment can help you gain clarity and insight into your thoughts and emotions.

Stress, anxiety, and negative self-talk are common challenges that many of us face. Recognizing the patterns and triggers of these challenges is crucial for developing effective coping strategies.

- **Identify Triggers**: Pay attention to the situations, people, or thoughts that trigger stress and anxiety. Understanding these triggers can help you prepare and respond more effectively.
- **Monitor Self-Talk**: Be mindful of your inner dialogue. Negative self-talk can be a major obstacle to personal growth. Challenge and reframe negative thoughts to foster a more positive mindset.

Setting specific, measurable goals is a vital step in overcoming personal challenges. Goals provide direction and purpose, and they help us track our progress.

- **Use the SMART Framework**: Set goals that are Specific, Measurable, Achievable, Relevant, and Time-bound. This framework ensures that your goals are clear and attainable.
- **Break Down Goals**: Break your larger goals into smaller, manageable tasks. This can make them less overwhelming and

more achievable.

- **Celebrate Progress**: Acknowledge and celebrate your progress, no matter how small. This can boost your motivation and confidence.

Identifying personal challenges and growth areas is a journey of self-discovery and empowerment. By embracing self-reflection, recognizing patterns of stress and negative self-talk, and setting specific, measurable goals, you can overcome obstacles and achieve a sense of balance and harmony in your life. Remember, the stars are there to guide you, but it's your willingness to grow and your resilience that will propel you forward on this journey.

Creating a Roadmap for Positive Change

Embarking on a journey of personal growth is akin to setting sail on a vast ocean of possibilities. To navigate these waters successfully, one needs a clear and actionable plan—a roadmap for positive change. This roadmap serves as a guiding light, illuminating the path toward achieving personal growth goals and overcoming life's challenges.

The first step in creating a roadmap for positive change is to develop a clear and actionable plan. This plan should outline your goals, the steps needed to achieve them, and the resources required along the way.

- **Define Your Goals**: Start by defining your goals. What do you want to achieve? Be as specific as possible. For example, instead of saying, "I want to be less stressed," say, "I want to practice mindfulness for 10 minutes every day to reduce stress."
- **Break Down Your Goals**: Break down your goals into smaller, achievable tasks. This makes the journey less

overwhelming and provides a sense of accomplishment as you complete each task.

- **Identify Resources**: Identify the resources you'll need to achieve your goals. This could include books, courses, support groups, or professional help.

Breaking down larger goals into smaller, manageable tasks is crucial for maintaining momentum and staying motivated. It's like climbing a mountain—one step at a time.

- **Set Mini-Goals**: Create mini-goals that lead up to your larger goal. Each mini-goal should be achievable within a short timeframe.
- **Celebrate Small Wins**: Celebrate each small win along the way. This reinforces positive behavior and keeps you motivated.
- **Adjust as Needed**: Be flexible and adjust your mini-goals as needed. Life is unpredictable, and being adaptable is key to success.

Setting realistic timelines and milestones is essential for tracking progress and staying on course. It provides structure and accountability, ensuring that you're moving in the right direction.

- **Create a Timeline**: Create a timeline for your goals, with specific deadlines for each task. This helps you stay organized and focused.
- **Establish Milestones**: Establish milestones to mark significant progress points. These milestones serve as checkpoints, allowing you to assess your progress and make adjustments if necessary.
- **Review and Reflect**: Regularly review your progress and

reflect on what you've learned. This can help you stay motivated and make necessary changes to your plan.

Creating a roadmap for positive change is a dynamic and empowering process. It requires clarity, organization, and a commitment to personal growth. By outlining steps, breaking down goals, and setting realistic timelines, you can navigate the journey of self-improvement with confidence and resilience. Remember, every step forward, no matter how small, is a step closer to achieving your goals and living a more fulfilling life.

Cultivating Mindfulness and Emotional Resilience

In the bustling rhythm of modern life, cultivating mindfulness and emotional resilience is akin to finding an oasis of calm in the midst of a storm. These invaluable tools empower us to navigate the challenges of life with grace, maintaining peace and equilibrium even in turbulent times. This section explores mindfulness techniques, the role of emotional resilience, and exercises for self-awareness and managing negative thoughts.

Mindfulness is the art of being present and fully engaged in the moment, without judgment. It's a practice that brings clarity, focus, and a deep sense of calm. Here are some techniques to incorporate mindfulness into your daily life:

- **Mindful Breathing**: Focus on your breath, noticing the sensation of air flowing in and out of your body. This simple practice can anchor you in the present moment and reduce stress.
- **Body Scan Meditation**: Starting from your toes and moving upwards, pay attention to each part of your body, noticing

any sensations, tensions, or relaxation. This helps you connect with your physical self and release tension.

- **Mindful Walking**: Take a leisurely walk, focusing on the sensation of your feet touching the ground. Observe the sights, sounds, and smells around you. This can be a refreshing way to practice mindfulness in nature.

Emotional resilience is the ability to adapt to and recover from emotional challenges. It's a cornerstone of mental well-being, enabling us to maintain peace and calm during turbulent times.

- **Acceptance**: Embrace your emotions without judgment. Accepting that it's okay to feel sad, anxious, or angry is the first step toward resilience.
- **Perspective**: Try to view challenges as opportunities for growth. This shift in perspective can transform obstacles into stepping stones.
- **Self-Care**: Prioritize activities that nourish your mind, body, and soul. Regular exercise, adequate sleep, and healthy eating contribute to emotional resilience.

Self-awareness is the foundation of emotional resilience. It involves understanding your thoughts, emotions, and behaviors. Here are some exercises to enhance self-awareness and manage negative thoughts:

- **Journaling**: Write down your thoughts and feelings. This can help you identify patterns and triggers of negative self-talk.
- **Cognitive Restructuring**: Challenge negative thoughts by asking yourself if they're based on facts or assumptions. Replace them with more positive and realistic statements.
- **Gratitude Practice**: Focus on the positive aspects of your life. Keeping a gratitude journal can shift your mindset from

negativity to appreciation.

Cultivating mindfulness and emotional resilience is a journey of self-discovery and growth. By practicing mindfulness techniques, embracing emotional resilience, and fostering self-awareness, you can navigate life's challenges with serenity and strength. Remember, the power to maintain peace and calm in the midst of chaos lies within you.

Achieving Balance and Harmony in Daily Life

In the symphony of life, achieving balance and harmony is akin to creating a beautiful melody that resonates with our innermost being. It's about finding the right rhythm and tempo that align with our personal values and priorities, allowing us to navigate life's pressures with grace and poise. This section explores strategies for creating a balanced lifestyle, setting boundaries, and integrating self-care routines and relaxation techniques into daily life.

A balanced lifestyle is one that harmonizes our physical, emotional, mental, and spiritual well-being. It's a lifestyle that aligns with our personal values and priorities, enabling us to live a fulfilling and meaningful life.

- **Identify Your Values**: Start by identifying your core values. What truly matters to you? Is it family, health, career, spirituality, or personal growth? Understanding your values helps you prioritize your time and energy.
- **Set Priorities**: Based on your values, set clear priorities. Allocate your time and resources to activities that align with these priorities and bring you joy and fulfillment.
- **Practice Moderation**: Balance is not about perfection. It's about practicing moderation and finding the middle ground

in all aspects of life, from work and leisure to socializing and solitude.

Setting boundaries is essential for managing life's pressures and maintaining balance. Boundaries help us define what we are comfortable with and how we want to be treated by others.

- **Communicate Your Boundaries**: Clearly communicate your boundaries to others. Whether it's saying no to additional work commitments or setting limits on social engagements, be assertive in expressing your needs.
- **Respect Your Own Boundaries**: It's important to respect your own boundaries. Honor your commitments to yourself, whether it's taking time off for relaxation or pursuing personal interests.
- **Be Flexible**: While it's important to have boundaries, be flexible when necessary. Life is unpredictable, and sometimes we need to adjust our boundaries to accommodate changing circumstances.

Self-care is the cornerstone of a balanced lifestyle. It's about taking care of your physical, emotional, and mental well-being through regular self-care routines and relaxation techniques.

- **Create a Self-Care Plan**: Develop a self-care plan that includes activities that nurture your body, mind, and soul. This could include regular exercise, healthy eating, meditation, journaling, or spending time in nature.
- **Incorporate Relaxation Techniques**: Incorporate relaxation techniques into your daily routine to reduce stress and promote relaxation. Techniques such as deep breathing, progressive muscle relaxation, or guided imagery can be

effective in calming the mind and body.

- **Make Time for Leisure**: Make time for leisure and activities that bring you joy. Whether it's reading a book, pursuing a hobby, or spending time with loved ones, leisure activities are vital for maintaining balance and harmony in life.

Achieving balance and harmony in daily life is a journey of self-discovery and intentional living. By creating a balanced lifestyle, setting boundaries, and integrating self-care routines and relaxation techniques, we can navigate the complexities of life with serenity and resilience. Remember, balance is not a destination, but a continuous process of aligning our lives with our true essence and purpose.

Adapting and Adjusting Goals for Sustainable Growth

In the journey of personal growth, the ability to adapt and adjust our goals is akin to a sailor adjusting the sails to navigate the changing winds. It's about embracing flexibility and adaptability in the goal-setting process, ensuring that our goals remain aligned with our evolving circumstances and aspirations. This section explores the importance of this adaptability, strategies for adjusting goals, and the value of celebrating progress and learning from setbacks.

Flexibility and adaptability are essential qualities in the goal-setting process. Life is unpredictable, and our plans often need to change in response to new information, unexpected challenges, or shifts in our priorities.

- **Stay Open to Change**: Cultivate an open mindset that welcomes change rather than resists it. This openness allows you to see new possibilities and opportunities that may arise.
- **Reassess Your Goals Regularly**: Make it a habit to regularly

reassess your goals. Are they still relevant and aligned with your values and aspirations? If not, it may be time to adjust them.

Life's unpredictability means that we often encounter situations that require us to adjust our goals. Whether it's a change in personal circumstances, a global event, or an unexpected opportunity, being able to pivot and adapt is crucial.

- **Identify What Needs to Change**: When circumstances change, take a step back and assess which aspects of your goals need adjustment. Is it the timeline, the scope, or the approach that needs to be revised?
- **Set Realistic Expectations**: Adjust your goals to reflect your current reality. This might mean setting smaller, more achievable goals or extending the timeline to accommodate new challenges.

The journey of self-improvement is not just about reaching the destination but also about celebrating the progress and learning from the setbacks along the way.

- **Acknowledge Your Achievements**: Take time to celebrate your achievements, no matter how small. These moments of celebration boost your morale and motivate you to keep moving forward.
- **Embrace Setbacks as Learning Opportunities**: Setbacks are an inevitable part of growth. Instead of viewing them as failures, see them as valuable learning experiences that can inform your future actions.

Adapting and adjusting goals for sustainable growth is a dynamic process that requires flexibility, resilience, and a positive outlook. By staying open to change, reassessing your goals regularly, and embracing both progress and setbacks, you can navigate the journey of personal growth with confidence and grace. Remember, it's not just about the destination but also about the growth and learning that occur along the way.

References

- Dweck, C. S. (2006). *Mindset: The New Psychology of Success*. Ballantine Books.
- Duckworth, A. (2016). *Grit: The Power of Passion and Perseverance*. Scribner.
- Kabat-Zinn, J. (1994). *Wherever You Go, There You Are: Mindfulness Meditation in Everyday Life*. Hyperion.
- Richardson, C. (1999). *Take Time for Your Life: A Personal Coach's 7-Step Program for Creating the Life You Want*. Broadway Books.
- Neff, K. D. (2011). *Self-Compassion: The Proven Power of Being Kind to Yourself*. William Morrow.
- Siegel, D. J. (2010). *Mindsight: The New Science of Personal Transformation*. Bantam.
- Covey, S. R. (1989). *The 7 Habits of Highly Effective People: Powerful Lessons in Personal Change*. Simon & Schuster.
- Duhigg, C. (2012). *The Power of Habit: Why We Do What We Do in Life and Business*. Random House.
- Clear, J. (2018). *Atomic Habits: An Easy & Proven Way to Build Good Habits & Break Bad Ones*. Penguin Random House.

- Seligman, M. E. P. (2002). *Authentic Happiness: Using the New Positive Psychology to Realize Your Potential for Lasting Fulfillment*. Free Press.

****

Chapter 10

The Calm After the Storm:

Maintaining Peace Amidst Change

In a world that is in constant flux, finding and maintaining peace amidst change is akin to discovering a beacon of light in the midst of a storm. It is a journey that requires adaptability, flexibility, and an unwavering commitment to inner tranquility. This chapter is dedicated to those who seek solace in the face of life's tempests, offering real-time tips and strategies for sustaining inner peace even as external circumstances shift and evolve.

Change is an inevitable part of life, yet it often brings with it overwhelming stress and anxiety. Whether it's personal or professional upheavals, the key to navigating these turbulent waters lies in embracing change as a constant. By accepting that change is a natural and unavoidable aspect of existence, we can begin to approach it with a sense of curiosity and openness, rather than fear and resistance.

- **Cultivate a Growth Mindset**: Adopt a growth mindset that views change as an opportunity for learning and personal development. This perspective can transform challenges into stepping stones, leading to greater resilience and adaptability.
- **Stay Grounded in the Present**: Practice mindfulness by staying anchored in the present moment. This can help mitigate anxiety about the future and regrets about the past, fostering a sense of calm and clarity.

Our inner dialogue plays a crucial role in how we perceive and respond to change. Negative thoughts and toxic self-talk can amplify our fears and create a barrier to peace. To counteract this, it's essential to cultivate a positive and compassionate inner voice.

- **Practice Self-Compassion**: Treat yourself with kindness and understanding, especially during challenging times. Acknowledge your feelings without judgment and offer yourself the same empathy you would extend to a friend.
- **Reframe Negative Thoughts**: When faced with negative thoughts, pause and challenge their validity. Reframe them in a more positive or realistic light, focusing on solutions and possibilities rather than problems and limitations.

In the midst of chaos, maintaining peace and calm can seem like an insurmountable task. However, with the right tools and techniques, it is possible to cultivate a sense of serenity that endures through life's storms.

- **Develop a Daily Calming Practice**: Incorporate practices such as meditation, deep breathing, or yoga into your daily routine. These activities can help center your mind and body, providing a refuge of calm in the midst of chaos.
- **Seek Solitude and Nature**: Spend time in solitude or immerse yourself in nature to reconnect with your inner self and the world around you. The tranquility of nature can be a powerful balm for a restless mind.

Achieving balance and harmony amidst change requires a conscious effort to align our lives with our values and priorities. It's about creating a sense of equilibrium that allows us to navigate life's pressures with grace and ease.

- **Set Boundaries**: Establish clear boundaries to protect your time, energy, and well-being. Learn to say no to demands that conflict with your values or deplete your resources.
- **Prioritize Self-Care**: Make self-care a priority. Nourish your body with healthy food, engage in regular physical activity, and ensure you get enough rest and relaxation.

By embracing change, navigating negative thoughts, maintaining calm, and striving for balance, we can weather life's storms with resilience and grace. Remember, peace is not the absence of turmoil but the ability to remain centered and composed in its midst.

Embracing Change with Open Arms

Change is an inevitable part of life. It can be as gentle as the shifting sands or as tumultuous as a stormy sea. Yet, it is in the heart of change that we find the seeds of growth and transformation. Embracing change with open arms is not just about acceptance; it's about recognizing the opportunities that lie within the challenges.

Change is a natural part of life. From the changing seasons to the cycles of our lives, change is ever-present. However, when faced with change, especially when it's unexpected or unwelcome, it can be a source of stress and anxiety. It's essential to understand that change is not an adversary but a constant companion on our journey.

- **Change as a Catalyst for Growth**: Every change, whether positive or negative, brings with it the opportunity for growth. It pushes us out of our comfort zones and challenges us to adapt and learn.
- **The Role of Perspective**: Our perspective on change can significantly impact how we experience it. Viewing change as

a threat can lead to resistance and fear, while seeing it as an opportunity can inspire creativity and resilience.

Embracing change requires a shift in mindset. It's about moving from a place of fear to a position of empowerment. Here are some strategies to help you view change as an opportunity for growth:

- **Cultivate a Growth Mindset**: Embrace the belief that your abilities and intelligence can develop through dedication and hard work. This mindset fosters a love for learning and resilience in the face of change.
- **Focus on the Possibilities**: Instead of dwelling on what you might lose, focus on what you might gain. Change often opens new doors and possibilities that we might not have considered before.
- **Practice Mindfulness**: Stay present in the moment. Mindfulness can help you navigate change with a sense of calm and clarity, reducing feelings of overwhelm and anxiety.
- **Seek Support**: Change can be daunting, but you don't have to face it alone. Seek support from friends, family, or professionals who can provide guidance and perspective.
- **Take Action**: Break down the change into manageable steps. Taking action, even small steps, can help you feel more in control and less at the mercy of the change.

For those struggling with overwhelming stress, anxiety, negative thoughts, and the need for balance, embracing change can be particularly challenging. However, it's in these moments that embracing change can be most transformative.

- **Reframe Negative Thoughts**: When faced with change, it's easy to fall into a pattern of negative thinking. Challenge these thoughts and reframe them in a more positive light.

- **Prioritize Self-Care**: Taking care of yourself is crucial during times of change. Prioritize activities that nurture your physical, emotional, and mental well-being.
- **Find Your Anchor**: In the midst of change, find something that remains constant. This could be a daily routine, a belief, or a practice that provides stability and comfort.

Embracing change with open arms is a journey of courage, resilience, and growth. It's about shifting our perspective, seeing the opportunities in the challenges, and taking proactive steps to navigate the winds of change. Remember, it's not the change itself that defines us, but how we respond to it.

Cultivating Inner Calm in Turbulent Times

In the whirlwind of life's challenges, cultivating inner calm is like finding a steady anchor amidst a storm. It's about nurturing a sense of serenity and peace within, even when the external world seems chaotic and unpredictable. This section explores techniques for maintaining inner peace and offers practical tips for staying centered through mindfulness, meditation, and deep breathing exercises.

Inner peace is not just a state of mind; it's a skill that can be cultivated and strengthened over time. Here are some techniques to help you maintain inner peace in turbulent times:

- **Mindful Awareness**: Practice mindful awareness by being present in the moment. Pay attention to your thoughts, feelings, and bodily sensations without judgment. This can help you stay grounded and centered amidst external chaos.
- **Positive Affirmations**: Use positive affirmations to reinforce

a sense of calm and positivity. Repeating phrases like "I am at peace" or "I am calm and centered" can help shift your mindset and reduce feelings of stress and anxiety.

Mindfulness and meditation are powerful tools for cultivating inner calm. They involve focusing your attention on the present moment, which can help quiet the mind and reduce stress.

- **Mindfulness Meditation**: Set aside a few minutes each day for mindfulness meditation. Find a quiet place, sit comfortably, and focus on your breath. When your mind wanders, gently bring your attention back to your breath.
- **Body Scan Meditation**: Practice body scan meditation to release tension and promote relaxation. Lie down or sit comfortably, and bring your awareness to different parts of your body, noticing any sensations or areas of tension.

Deep breathing exercises are a simple yet effective way to cultivate inner calm. They can help activate the body's relaxation response and reduce feelings of stress and anxiety.

- **Diaphragmatic Breathing**: Place one hand on your chest and the other on your belly. Breathe in deeply through your nose, allowing your belly to rise more than your chest. Exhale slowly through your mouth, letting your belly fall.
- **4-7-8 Breathing Technique**: Inhale deeply through your nose for a count of 4, hold your breath for a count of 7, and exhale slowly through your mouth for a count of 8. Repeat this cycle several times.

Cultivating inner calm in turbulent times is a journey of self-discovery and practice. By incorporating mindfulness, meditation, and deep breathing exercises into your daily routine, you can develop a sense of peace and tranquility that endures through life's challenges. Remember, inner calm is not about escaping the storm, but about finding peace within it.

Navigating Negative Thoughts and Self-Talk

In the journey of life, negative thoughts and toxic self-talk can be formidable obstacles, casting shadows over our peace and tranquility. Addressing and transforming these negative thinking patterns into more positive and constructive ones is essential for maintaining inner calm amidst change. This section offers strategies to help you navigate the challenges of negative thoughts and self-talk, fostering a more positive mindset.

Negative thoughts and self-talk are often automatic and can stem from past experiences, fears, or insecurities. They can manifest as critical inner voices that undermine our confidence and well-being.

- **Recognize the Patterns**: Begin by recognizing the patterns of your negative thoughts and self-talk. Are they related to specific situations or themes, such as fear of failure or feelings of inadequacy?
- **Acknowledge Their Impact**: Acknowledge the impact that negative thoughts and self-talk have on your emotions and behavior. Understanding this connection is the first step towards change.

Transforming negative thinking patterns requires practice and persistence. Here are some strategies to help you shift towards a more positive and constructive mindset:

- **Challenge Negative Thoughts**: When a negative thought arises, challenge its validity. Ask yourself, "Is this thought based on facts or assumptions?" and "What evidence do I have to support or refute this thought?"
- **Reframe Your Thoughts**: Practice reframing negative thoughts into more positive or neutral statements. For example, instead of thinking, "I'll never be good enough," reframe it to, "I am doing my best and learning every day."
- **Focus on Solutions**: Instead of dwelling on problems, shift your focus to finding solutions. This proactive approach can help reduce feelings of helplessness and boost your confidence.

Creating a positive inner dialogue is an ongoing process that can significantly enhance your mental and emotional well-being.

- **Practice Self-Compassion**: Treat yourself with kindness and understanding, just as you would a friend. Remind yourself that everyone makes mistakes and that you are deserving of compassion.
- **Use Positive Affirmations**: Incorporate positive affirmations into your daily routine. Repeating affirmations such as "I am capable and strong" or "I am worthy of love and happiness" can help reinforce a positive self-image.
- **Celebrate Your Strengths**: Focus on your strengths and achievements. Celebrating your positive qualities can help counteract negative self-talk and build self-esteem.

Navigating negative thoughts and self-talk is a crucial aspect of maintaining peace amidst change. By understanding the patterns of negative thinking, challenging and reframing these thoughts, and cultivating a positive inner dialogue, you can transform your mindset and embrace a more optimistic outlook on life. Remember, the power to change your thoughts lies within you, and each step towards positivity is a step towards peace.

Finding Balance Amidst Life's Pressures

In the fast-paced rhythm of modern life, finding balance amidst life's pressures is akin to discovering harmony in a symphony. It's about orchestrating the various aspects of our lives – personal, professional, emotional, and physical – in a way that promotes peace and well-being. This section explores the importance of balance and offers tips for achieving harmony through prioritization and time management.

Balance is the cornerstone of a peaceful and fulfilling life. It's about creating equilibrium between work and leisure, action and rest, giving and receiving. When our lives are balanced, we experience a sense of harmony and flow, which contributes to our overall well-being.

- **Holistic Well-Being**: Balance is not just about managing time; it's about nurturing all aspects of our being – physical, emotional, mental, and spiritual.
- **Reducing Stress and Anxiety**: Achieving balance helps reduce stress and anxiety by preventing overcommitment and burnout. It allows us to allocate time for relaxation and self-care.

Finding harmony in both personal and professional life is essential for sustained peace and happiness. It involves setting clear priorities and managing time effectively.

- **Set Clear Priorities**: Identify what truly matters to you. What are your core values and goals? Prioritizing these aspects of your life can help you allocate your time and energy more effectively.

- **Time Management**: Use time management tools and techniques to organize your schedule. Allocate specific times for work, leisure, self-care, and social activities. Avoid multitasking, as it can lead to stress and decreased productivity.

Finding balance is a dynamic process that requires ongoing attention and adjustment. Here are some practical tips to help you find and maintain balance:

- **Learn to Say No**: Recognize your limits and learn to say no to additional commitments that don't align with your priorities or that may overwhelm you.
- **Practice Mindfulness**: Engage in mindfulness practices to stay present and focused. This can help you make more conscious choices about how you spend your time.
- **Seek Support**: Don't hesitate to seek support from friends, family, or professionals when you're struggling to find balance. Sometimes, an outside perspective can provide valuable insights.
- **Regular Check-ins**: Regularly assess your life balance and make adjustments as needed. Life is ever-changing, and what worked for you in the past may not work now.
- **Embrace Flexibility**: Be open to change and flexible in your approach. Balance doesn't mean rigidity; it means adapting to life's ebb and flow.

Finding balance amidst life's pressures is an essential component of maintaining peace and well-being. By setting clear priorities, managing time effectively, and embracing flexibility, you can create a harmonious life that allows you to thrive both personally and professionally. Remember, balance is not a destination but a continuous journey of adjustment and alignment.

Building Resilience for Sustainable Peace

In a world that is constantly changing, resilience is the key to navigating life's storms and maintaining a sense of peace amidst the chaos. Resilience is the ability to adapt to change, overcome challenges, and bounce back stronger than before. This section highlights the role of resilience in adapting to change and provides insights into developing emotional and mental resilience for long-term inner peace.

Change is an inevitable part of life, and our ability to adapt to it is what defines our resilience. Resilience allows us to face change with courage and flexibility, turning obstacles into opportunities for growth.

- **Embracing Change**: Resilient individuals see change as an integral part of life's journey. They embrace change with a positive attitude, seeing it as a chance to learn and evolve.
- **Flexibility and Adaptability**: Flexibility is at the heart of resilience. It's about being open to new experiences and adaptable in the face of change. This flexibility helps maintain peace and stability even when the external world is in flux.

Emotional and mental resilience are the foundations of sustainable peace. They empower us to manage stress, navigate negative thoughts, and maintain balance amidst life's pressures.

- **Cultivating Emotional Awareness**: Understanding and managing your emotions is crucial for resilience. Practice emotional awareness by acknowledging your feelings, exploring their origins, and expressing them in healthy ways.

- **Building Mental Strength**: Mental resilience involves developing a strong and positive mindset. It's about focusing on solutions, learning from setbacks, and maintaining a hopeful outlook on life.
- **Practicing Self-Care**: Self-care is vital for resilience. Engage in activities that nourish your body, mind, and soul, such as exercise, meditation, and spending time in nature.

Building resilience is a continuous process that requires dedication and practice. Here are some strategies to help you develop resilience and sustain peace:

- **Establish Support Networks**: Surround yourself with supportive friends and family who can provide encouragement and perspective during tough times.
- **Set Realistic Goals**: Set achievable goals that align with your values and aspirations. This gives you a sense of purpose and direction, which is essential for resilience.
- **Learn from Challenges**: View challenges as opportunities for growth. Reflect on your experiences, learn from them, and use them to strengthen your resilience.

Building resilience for sustainable peace is about embracing change, developing emotional and mental strength, and practicing self-care. By cultivating resilience, you can navigate life's challenges with grace and maintain a sense of inner peace and harmony, even in turbulent times.

References

- Southwick, S. M., & Charney, D. S. (2012). *Resilience: The Science of*

Mastering Life's Greatest Challenges. Cambridge University Press.

- Reivich, K., & Shatté, A. (2002). *The Resilience Factor: 7 Keys to Finding Your Inner Strength and Overcoming Life's Hurdles.* Broadway Books.
- Fredrickson, B. L. (2009). *Positivity: Top-Notch Research Reveals the Upward Spiral That Will Change Your Life.* Crown Publishing Group.
- Allen, D. (2001). *Getting Things Done: The Art of Stress-Free Productivity.* Penguin Books.
- Burns, D. D. (1999). *Feeling Good: The New Mood Therapy.* HarperCollins Publishers.
- Thich Nhat Hanh. (1992). *Peace Is Every Step: The Path of Mindfulness in Everyday Life.* Bantam Books.
- Harris, D. (2014). *10% Happier: How I Tamed the Voice in My Head, Reduced Stress Without Losing My Edge, and Found Self-Help That Actually Works.* HarperCollins.
- Covey, S. R. (1989). *The 7 Habits of Highly Effective People: Powerful Lessons in Personal Change.* Simon & Schuster.
- Dweck, C. S. (2006). *Mindset: The New Psychology of Success.* Ballantine Books.
- Kabat-Zinn, J. (1994). *Wherever You Go, There You Are: Mindfulness Meditation in Everyday Life.* Hyperion.
- Neff, K. D. (2011). *Self-Compassion: The Proven Power of Being Kind to Yourself.* William Morrow.

****

Chapter 11

Harboring Gratitude:

The Role of Thankfulness in Healing

In the tapestry of life, gratitude is the golden thread that weaves together moments of joy, contentment, and peace. It is the practice of recognizing and appreciating the good in our lives, even amidst challenges and adversity. In this chapter, "Harboring Gratitude: The Role of Thankfulness in Healing," we will explore the transformative power of gratitude in enhancing mental health and fostering a positive outlook, offering solace to those who struggle with overwhelming stress, negative thoughts, and the quest for balance in turbulent times.

Gratitude is more than a mere feeling; it is a potent force that can reshape our mental landscape, turning obstacles into opportunities and despair into hope. By focusing on what we are thankful for, we shift our attention away from life's stresses and towards its blessings, nurturing a sense of abundance and well-being.

Embracing gratitude involves consciously acknowledging the good in our lives, from the simple pleasures to the profound gifts. It's about savoring the present moment and recognizing the beauty that surrounds us.

Research has shown that practicing gratitude can lead to significant improvements in mental health, reducing symptoms of depression and anxiety, and enhancing overall happiness and life satisfaction.

In the midst of overwhelming stress and anxiety, gratitude can serve as a beacon of light, guiding us through the darkness. It empowers us to reframe our challenges, viewing them not as insurmountable obstacles but as opportunities for growth and learning.

Even in the hardest of times, there are always things to be grateful for. It might be the support of loved ones, the beauty of nature, or the resilience of the human spirit.

By focusing on gratitude, we can create a buffer against negative thoughts and toxic self-talk, fostering a more positive and resilient mindset.

To harness the full power of gratitude, it's essential to integrate it into our daily routines. This can be done through simple practices that encourage mindfulness and thankfulness.

Writing down a few things you're grateful for each day can help solidify the habit of gratitude and provide a source of comfort during tough times.

Incorporating gratitude rituals into your daily life, such as expressing thanks before meals or sharing gratitude with loved ones, can help reinforce a thankful mindset.

By cultivating a grateful heart, we can navigate life's storms with greater ease and emerge with a deeper appreciation for the beauty and blessings that abound. Let us embrace gratitude as a healing balm, a source of strength, and a pathway to peace.

The Science of Gratitude and Mental Well-Being

In recent years, the study of gratitude has gained significant attention in the field of positive psychology, with researchers exploring its profound impact on mental well-being. Gratitude, defined as the appreciation of what is valuable and meaningful to oneself, has been shown to be a powerful tool in reducing stress, anxiety, and depression, as well as rewiring the brain to focus on positive experiences and emotions.

A growing body of research demonstrates that practicing gratitude can lead to significant improvements in mental health. In a study by Emmons and McCullough (2003), participants who kept a weekly gratitude journal reported fewer physical symptoms, felt better about their lives as a whole, and were more optimistic about the upcoming week compared to those who recorded hassles or neutral life events. This suggests that gratitude can effectively reduce stress and enhance overall well-being.

Gratitude has also been shown to play a role in reducing symptoms of anxiety and depression. A study by Wood et al. (2010) found that gratitude was associated with lower levels of depression and anxiety, higher levels of subjective well-being, and better sleep quality. By focusing on positive aspects of life, gratitude helps to shift attention away from negative emotions and thoughts that often accompany anxiety and depression.

Neuroscientific research has begun to uncover how gratitude can rewire the brain to focus on positive experiences and emotions. The practice of gratitude has been linked to increased activity in the prefrontal cortex, the area of the brain associated with positive emotion and decision-making. This suggests that gratitude can enhance the brain's capacity for joy and contentment.

Furthermore, gratitude has been shown to increase the production of neurotransmitters such as serotonin and dopamine, which are known as the "feel-good" chemicals in the brain. This increase in positive neurotransmitters can lead to a more optimistic outlook on life and a greater sense of happiness.

The science of gratitude offers valuable insights for individuals struggling with stress, negative thoughts, and challenges in maintaining peace and balance. By incorporating gratitude practices into daily life, such as keeping a gratitude journal, expressing thanks to others, or reflecting on positive experiences, individuals can enhance their mental well-being and resilience.

Gratitude can also serve as a coping mechanism during turbulent times, providing a sense of hope and perspective when faced with adversity. By focusing on the things we are thankful for, we can cultivate a sense of inner calm and stability amidst the chaos.

The science of gratitude and mental well-being is a testament to the transformative power of thankfulness in healing. By understanding the impact of gratitude on reducing stress, anxiety, and depression, and exploring how it can rewire the brain to focus on positive experiences, we can harness this powerful tool to enhance our mental health and foster a positive outlook on life. Embracing gratitude is a step toward harboring a sense of peace and well-being in our lives.

Cultivating Gratitude in Daily Life

In the tapestry of our daily lives, cultivating gratitude is like weaving threads of joy, appreciation, and contentment into our everyday routines. It's a practice that can transform our perspective, enhance our well-being, and bring a sense of peace amidst life's challenges. This section provides practical tips for integrating gratitude practices into everyday routines and highlights the importance of mindfulness in recognizing moments of gratitude.

Integrating gratitude into our daily lives can be simple and rewarding. Dedicate a few minutes each day to write down things you are thankful for. It could be as simple as a warm cup of coffee, a kind gesture from a friend, or the beauty of a sunset. Reflecting on these moments can enhance your appreciation for life's blessings.

Make it a habit to express gratitude to others. A simple "thank you" to a colleague, a note of appreciation to a loved one, or a kind word to a stranger can spread positivity and strengthen relationships.

Set reminders on your phone or place sticky notes in visible areas to prompt you to think about what you're grateful for throughout the day. These reminders can help you stay focused on gratitude even during busy or stressful times.

Mindfulness is the practice of being present and fully engaged in the moment. It plays a crucial role in recognizing and savoring moments of gratitude.

Take time to observe your surroundings and experiences with a sense of curiosity and openness. Mindful observation can help you notice and appreciate the beauty and goodness in everyday life.

Incorporate gratitude meditation into your routine. Focus on feeling grateful for the breath in your lungs, the body that supports you, and the people and experiences that enrich your life.

Practice gratitude while eating by paying attention to the flavors, textures, and origins of your food. Appreciate the nourishment it provides and the effort that went into its preparation.

For those struggling with stress, negative thoughts, and maintaining balance, gratitude can be a powerful tool for shifting perspective and finding peace.

Even in challenging times, there are things to be grateful for. Focusing on these can provide a sense of hope and resilience.

When negative thoughts arise, counteract them by thinking of something you're grateful for. This can help break the cycle of negativity and foster a more positive mindset.

In the quest for balance and harmony, gratitude can be a grounding force, reminding us of what truly matters and helping us prioritize our well-being.

Cultivating gratitude in daily life is a journey of appreciation, mindfulness, and transformation. By integrating gratitude practices into our routines and embracing mindfulness, we can enhance our mental health, foster a positive outlook, and navigate life's pressures with grace and gratitude. Let us embrace the practice of thankfulness as a pathway to healing and peace.

Gratitude as a Tool for Overcoming Negative Thoughts

In the realm of personal growth and healing, gratitude emerges as a powerful tool for overcoming negative thoughts and toxic thinking patterns. By shifting our focus from what is lacking to what is abundant in our lives, gratitude can transform our perspective and foster a sense of contentment and peace. This section explores strategies for using gratitude to counteract negative self-talk and offers insights into the transformative power of thankfulness.

Negative self-talk and toxic thinking patterns can be pervasive, influencing our emotions and behaviors in detrimental ways. Gratitude can serve as an antidote, helping to reframe our thoughts and cultivate a more positive mindset.

When negative thoughts arise, acknowledge them without judgment. Then, challenge their validity by asking yourself whether they are based on facts or distorted perceptions. Gratitude can help you focus on the positive aspects of your life, providing a counterbalance to negative thinking.

Make gratitude a daily practice. Set aside time each day to reflect on things you are thankful for, no matter how small. This consistent practice can gradually shift your focus from negative to positive, reducing the power of toxic self-talk.

Gratitude has the remarkable ability to shift our focus from what we lack to what we possess. By appreciating the abundance in our lives, we can foster a sense of contentment and well-being.

Instead of focusing on what you don't have, practice seeing the abundance around you. Gratitude helps you recognize the wealth of blessings in your life, from meaningful relationships to simple pleasures.

Gratitude encourages us to savor positive experiences and moments of joy. By fully appreciating these moments, we can create a reservoir of positivity that can help dilute the impact of negative thoughts.

Incorporating gratitude into your daily life can take many forms. Keep a gratitude journal where you write down things you're thankful for each day. This practice can help you become more aware of the positive aspects of your life and reduce negative thinking.

Engage in gratitude meditation, where you focus on feelings of thankfulness and appreciation. This can help calm your mind and reduce stress and anxiety.

Regularly express gratitude to others. This not only strengthens your relationships but also reinforces your own sense of gratitude.

Gratitude is a powerful tool for overcoming negative thoughts and toxic thinking patterns. By practicing gratitude daily and integrating it into our lives, we can shift our focus from what is lacking to what is abundant, fostering a sense of peace and contentment. Embracing gratitude is a step toward healing and a more positive outlook on life.

The Role of Gratitude in Building Resilience

In the face of life's challenges, resilience is the inner strength that allows us to bounce back, adapt, and thrive. Gratitude, the practice of recognizing and appreciating the positive aspects of life, plays a crucial role in building and sustaining this resilience. This section explores how gratitude can strengthen emotional resilience and discusses the connection between gratitude and coping mechanisms that support long-term mental health.

Emotional resilience is the ability to navigate through difficult emotions and situations without losing one's sense of purpose and inner peace. Gratitude can significantly contribute to this resilience in several ways.

Gratitude naturally evokes positive emotions such as joy, contentment, and love. These positive emotions can create a buffer against stress and adversity, helping individuals to maintain a balanced emotional state.

By focusing on what is good in our lives, gratitude helps shift our perspective from dwelling on problems to appreciating the blessings. This shift in focus can reduce feelings of helplessness and despair, fostering a more resilient outlook.

Expressing gratitude strengthens relationships and builds social support, which is a key component of resilience. Feeling connected and supported can provide comfort and strength during tough times.

Gratitude is not only a short-term mood booster but also a powerful tool for developing coping mechanisms that support long-term mental health.

Gratitude encourages cognitive reframing, a coping strategy that involves changing the way we perceive and interpret stressful situations. By focusing on the positive, gratitude can help reframe challenges as opportunities for growth.

Regular practice of gratitude has been linked to lower levels of stress hormones such as cortisol. By reducing stress, gratitude contributes to overall mental health and well-being.

Research has shown that gratitude can play a significant role in resilience following traumatic events. By finding things to be thankful for even in the midst of trauma, individuals can foster hope and healing.

Regularly write down things you are grateful for. This practice can help you notice and appreciate the positive aspects of your life, even during challenging times.

Engage in gratitude meditation, focusing on feelings of thankfulness and appreciation. This can help calm the mind and strengthen emotional resilience.

Make a habit of expressing gratitude to others. This not only strengthens relationships but also reinforces your own sense of gratitude and resilience.

Gratitude is a powerful ally in building resilience and maintaining long-term mental health. By fostering positive emotions, shifting perspective, and developing effective coping mechanisms, gratitude can help us navigate life's challenges with grace and strength. Embracing gratitude is a step toward a more resilient and fulfilling life.

Fostering Gratitude in Relationships and Communities

In the tapestry of human experience, relationships and communities are the threads that bind us together, providing support, connection, and a sense of belonging. Gratitude plays a pivotal role in strengthening these social bonds, enhancing empathy, and fostering harmony. This section highlights the role of gratitude in enhancing social connections and discusses how expressing gratitude can improve relationships and foster a sense of belonging and harmony.

Gratitude is a powerful force in building and maintaining strong, healthy relationships. It encourages us to focus on the positive aspects of our interactions with others, leading to deeper connections and mutual appreciation.

Expressing gratitude to those around us strengthens our bonds with them. It acknowledges their value in our lives and reinforces the positive behaviors that contribute to healthy relationships.

Gratitude enhances empathy, the ability to understand and share the feelings of others. When we appreciate the kindness and efforts of others, we are more likely to respond with empathy and compassion in our interactions.

Expressing gratitude is a simple yet profound way to improve relationships and foster a sense of belonging and harmony within communities.

Incorporate gratitude into your daily communication. A simple "thank you" can go a long way in acknowledging someone's efforts and making them feel appreciated.

Publicly acknowledging the contributions of others, whether in a family gathering, a team meeting, or a community event, can create a culture of gratitude and recognition.

Gratitude not only benefits individual relationships but also has a positive impact on the well-being of entire communities.

Gratitude can help build strong support networks within communities. When people feel appreciated, they are more likely to offer their support and assistance to others in times of need.

Gratitude fosters a sense of harmony and cooperation in communities. By focusing on the positive and expressing thankfulness, communities can create an atmosphere of mutual respect and understanding.

Even in the face of overwhelming stress and challenges, gratitude can be a beacon of hope and a tool for healing in relationships and communities.

Practicing gratitude in difficult times can build resilience, helping individuals and communities to bounce back from adversity and maintain peace and calm.

In turbulent times, finding gratitude in small things can make a significant difference. It can shift the focus from what is lacking to what is present and valuable in our lives and relationships.

Fostering gratitude in relationships and communities is a journey of appreciation, connection, and healing. By highlighting the role of gratitude in enhancing social connections and expressing gratitude to improve relationships, we can create a ripple effect of positivity, empathy, and harmony. Embracing gratitude is a step toward building stronger bonds and fostering a sense of belonging in our lives and the world around us.

References

- Algoe, S. B. (2012). *Find, Remind, and Bind: The Functions of Gratitude in Everyday Relationships.* Social and Personality Psychology Compass, 6(6), 455-469.
- Froh, J. J., & Bono, G. (2014). *Making Grateful Kids: The Science of Building Character.* Templeton Press.
- Southwick, S. M., & Charney, D. S. (2012). *Resilience: The Science of Mastering Life's Greatest Challenges.* Cambridge University Press.
- Fredrickson, B. L. (2009). *Positivity: Top-Notch Research Reveals the Upward Spiral That Will Change Your Life.* Crown Publishing Group.
- Watkins, P. C. (2014). *Gratitude and the Good Life: Toward a Psychology of Appreciation.* Springer.
- Kabat-Zinn, J. (1994). *Wherever You Go, There You Are: Mindfulness Meditation in Everyday Life.* Hyperion.
- Neff, K. D. (2011). *Self-Compassion: The Proven Power of Being Kind to Yourself.* William Morrow.
- Wood, A. M., Froh, J. J., & Geraghty, A. W. A. (2010). *Gratitude and well-being: A review and theoretical integration.* Clinical Psychology Review, 30(7), 890-905.
- Emmons, R. A., & McCullough, M. E. (2003). *Counting blessings versus burdens: An experimental investigation of gratitude and subjective well-being in daily life.* Journal of Personality and Social Psychology, 84(2), 377-389.
- Seligman, M. E. P., Steen, T. A., Park, N., & Peterson, C. (2005). *Positive psychology progress: Empirical validation of interventions.* American Psychologist, 60(5), 410-421.

****

Chapter 12

Embarking on Your Journey:

Creating Your Personal Peace Plan

In the voyage of life, each of us yearns for a sanctuary of tranquility, a haven of inner peace amidst the tumult of everyday existence. "Embarking on Your Journey: Creating Your Personal Peace Plan" is a chapter dedicated to guiding you on a path toward achieving and sustaining this coveted state of serenity. It offers a step-by-step approach to developing a personalized plan that addresses the unique challenges you face, providing practical strategies to navigate the waters of stress, anxiety, and imbalance.

In a world where stress and anxiety are prevalent, finding inner peace is more important than ever. Whether it's the pressures of work, the challenges of personal relationships, or the constant barrage of negative thoughts, these factors can disrupt our sense of calm and balance. A personal peace plan is a proactive approach to managing these stressors, helping you cultivate a sense of tranquility that endures through life's ups and downs.

The first step in creating your personal peace plan is to lay a solid foundation. This involves taking time to reflect on your current state of mind. What are your primary sources of stress and anxiety? What negative thoughts or self-talk patterns do you struggle with?

Define what inner peace means to you. What are your goals for emotional and mental well-being? Setting clear intentions will guide your journey and help you stay focused on your objectives.

Your personal peace plan should be tailored to your individual needs and circumstances. Here are some essential building blocks to consider:

- **Mindfulness and Meditation**: Incorporate mindfulness and meditation practices into your daily routine. These techniques can help you stay present, reduce stress, and foster a sense of inner calm.
- **Gratitude Practice**: Cultivate an attitude of gratitude. Regularly expressing thankfulness for the positive aspects of your life can shift your focus from what's lacking to what's abundant, enhancing your overall sense of well-being.
- **Stress Management Techniques**: Identify and implement stress management techniques that work for you. This could include deep breathing exercises, physical activity, or engaging in hobbies that bring you joy.

Creating your personal peace plan is just the beginning. Make a commitment to practice the elements of your peace plan consistently. Consistency is crucial for building habits that support long-term well-being. Be open to adjusting your plan as needed. Life is dynamic, and your peace plan should be flexible enough to accommodate changes and challenges that arise.

By developing a personalized plan that addresses your unique challenges, you can cultivate a sense of inner peace that not only enhances your quality of life but also enables you to navigate life's storms with grace and resilience. Remember, the journey to inner peace is ongoing, and each step you take is a step toward a more balanced and fulfilling life.

Assessing Your Current State

Embarking on your journey toward inner peace begins with a candid assessment of your current state. This introspective process involves reflecting on your levels of stress, anxiety, and overall well-being, and identifying the sources of your stress and the areas of your life where you seek more peace and balance. By understanding your starting point, you can tailor your personal peace plan to address your specific needs and challenges.

Begin by taking a moment to evaluate your current emotional landscape. Ask yourself, how often do I feel stressed or anxious? Consider the frequency of your stress and anxiety. Is it a constant presence, or does it come in waves?

What are the physical and emotional symptoms I experience? Identify the physical sensations (such as tension, headaches, or fatigue) and emotional responses (such as irritability, sadness, or worry) associated with your stress and anxiety.

How do these feelings impact my daily life? Reflect on how stress and anxiety affect your relationships, work, and overall quality of life.

To effectively manage stress, it's crucial to pinpoint its origins. Consider the various aspects of your life and identify the specific factors that contribute to your stress and anxiety:

- **Personal Life**: Are there issues in your relationships, health, or personal goals that are causing stress?
- **Professional Life**: Examine your work environment, job responsibilities, and career aspirations for potential stressors.
- **Environmental Factors**: Consider external factors such as social, political, or economic conditions that might be contributing to your stress.

Once you've identified the sources of your stress, turn your focus to the areas of your life where you desire more peace and balance.

Assess your physical health and lifestyle habits. Are there changes you can make to improve your physical well-being and reduce stress?

Reflect on your emotional health and coping mechanisms. What practices can you adopt to cultivate emotional resilience and inner peace?

Consider the quality of your relationships. How can you foster more harmonious and supportive connections with others?

To help you facilitate this self-assessment process, consider keeping a journal to record your thoughts, feelings, and experiences related to stress and anxiety. This can help you identify patterns and triggers over time.

Engage in mindfulness practices such as meditation or deep breathing exercises to enhance self-awareness and promote a sense of calm.

Sometimes, an outside perspective can provide valuable insights. Consider seeking feedback from trusted friends, family members, or a mental health professional.

Assessing your current state is the first step in creating your personal peace plan. By reflecting on your levels of stress and anxiety, identifying the sources of your stress, and seeking areas for peace and balance, you can lay the groundwork for a journey toward inner peace. Remember, this assessment is not about judgment but about understanding and compassion for yourself as you embark on this transformative path.

Setting Clear Goals for Inner Peace

Embarking on your journey to inner peace begins with setting clear and meaningful goals for your emotional and mental well-being. This process involves defining what inner peace means to you and identifying specific, achievable objectives that will guide your path. In this section, we'll explore how to set these goals and the importance of realistic expectations and self-compassion throughout your journey.

Inner peace is a personal and unique experience, varying from one individual to another. To set meaningful goals, start by reflecting on what inner peace means to you.

Does inner peace mean feeling calm and centered, even in the face of challenges?

Is it about having a clear mind, free from clutter and negative thoughts?

Does it involve finding a sense of balance and harmony in your life?

Once you have a clear understanding of what inner peace means to you, it's time to set specific and achievable goals. These goals should be tailored to your personal needs and aspirations.

Set a goal to reduce stress through specific practices such as meditation, yoga, or deep breathing exercises.

Aim to cultivate a more positive mindset by challenging negative thoughts and practicing gratitude.

Set a goal to build emotional resilience by developing coping strategies for dealing with difficult emotions.

Setting realistic expectations is crucial for maintaining motivation and avoiding disappointment. Recognize that inner peace is a journey, not a destination, and progress may be gradual.

Break your goals into smaller, manageable steps to make them more achievable.

Celebrate each small victory along the way, acknowledging your progress and effort.

Be open to adjusting your goals if you find that they are not serving you or if your circumstances change.

Self-compassion is a vital component of your journey to inner peace. Being kind to yourself throughout this process is essential.

Treat yourself with kindness and understanding, especially when faced with setbacks or challenges.

Refrain from harsh self-criticism and instead focus on self-encouragement and positive reinforcement.

Don't hesitate to seek support from friends, family, or professionals if you need it. You don't have to embark on this journey alone.

Setting clear goals for inner peace is a critical first step in your journey toward emotional and mental well-being. By defining what inner peace means to you, setting specific and achievable goals, maintaining realistic expectations, and practicing self-compassion, you can navigate the path to inner peace with confidence and grace. Remember, this journey is about progress, not perfection, and each step forward is a step toward a more peaceful and fulfilling life.

Developing Mindfulness and Self-Awareness

In the quest for inner peace, developing mindfulness and self-awareness is paramount. Mindfulness is the practice of being fully present and engaged in the moment, while self-awareness involves understanding your thoughts, emotions, and behaviors. Together, they form a powerful duo that can help you navigate life's challenges with grace and clarity. This section provides techniques for cultivating mindfulness and highlights the role of self-awareness in recognizing and managing negative thoughts and toxic self-talk.

Mindfulness can be cultivated through various practices and techniques that encourage you to focus on the present moment without judgment.

Set aside a few minutes each day to sit quietly and focus on your breath. When your mind wanders, gently bring your attention back to your breathing.

Deep breathing is a simple yet effective way to reduce stress and promote mindfulness. Try the 4-7-8 technique: inhale for 4 seconds, hold for 7 seconds, and exhale for 8 seconds.

Practice observing your surroundings with a sense of curiosity and openness. Pay attention to the sights, sounds, and smells around you, and notice how they make you feel.

A body scan is a mindfulness exercise that involves paying attention to different parts of your body in turn, noticing any sensations or tensions.

Self-awareness is crucial in recognizing and managing negative thoughts and toxic self-talk. By becoming more aware of your inner dialogue, you can challenge and reframe negative patterns.

Pay attention to your thoughts and identify patterns of negativity or self-criticism. Write them down to gain a clearer understanding of your mental habits.

Once you've identified negative thoughts, challenge their validity. Ask yourself if they're based on facts or assumptions and consider alternative, more positive perspectives.

Treat yourself with kindness and understanding. Remind yourself that everyone makes mistakes and that you're doing the best you can.

To make mindfulness and self-awareness part of your daily routine, consider dedicating a specific time each day for mindfulness practice, whether it's meditation, deep breathing, or mindful observation.

Incorporate mindfulness cues into your day, such as taking a deep breath every time you check your phone or practicing mindful observation during your commute.

Spend a few minutes each evening reflecting on your day. Consider what went well, what you're grateful for, and how you managed any challenges.

Developing mindfulness and self-awareness is a journey that requires patience, practice, and compassion. By incorporating mindfulness techniques into your daily life and cultivating self-awareness, you can enhance your ability to manage stress, navigate negative thoughts, and maintain a sense of peace and balance. Embrace this journey with an open heart, and watch as your personal peace plan unfolds.

Creating a Personalized Peace Plan

Embarking on your journey to inner peace is a deeply personal and transformative process. Creating a personalized peace plan is about bringing together the insights and strategies from your self-assessment, goal-setting, mindfulness practices, and self-awareness work into a cohesive plan that addresses your unique needs and challenges. This section will guide you through the process of creating and maintaining your personalized peace plan.

To create your personalized peace plan, start by reviewing the insights and strategies you've gathered from the previous sections.

Reflect on your levels of stress, anxiety, and overall well-being. Identify the sources of your stress and the areas where you seek more peace and balance.

Define what inner peace means to you and set specific, achievable goals for your emotional and mental well-being.

Incorporate mindfulness and self-awareness practices into your plan to enhance your ability to stay present and manage negative thoughts.

Your personal peace plan should be structured in a way that is clear, achievable, and flexible.

Outline the daily practices you will engage in to cultivate inner peace, such as meditation, deep breathing, or gratitude journaling.

Include specific techniques you will use to manage stress and anxiety, such as mindfulness exercises or physical activity.

List the coping strategies you will employ when faced with challenges, such as seeking support from friends or using positive affirmations.

Your personal peace plan is a living document that should evolve with you as you grow and change. Regularly review and adjust your plan to ensure it remains relevant and effective.

Schedule regular check-ins with yourself to review your progress and make any necessary adjustments to your plan.

Be open to modifying your plan as your needs and circumstances change. Flexibility is key to maintaining a plan that supports your well-being.

Acknowledge and celebrate your progress, no matter how small. Recognizing your achievements can motivate you to continue your path to inner peace.

Creating a personalized peace plan is a powerful step in your journey to inner peace. By combining insights and strategies, structuring your plan, and regularly reviewing and adjusting it, you can develop a roadmap that supports your emotional and mental well-being. Embrace this process with an open heart and a commitment to self-care, as well as watch while you cultivate a sense of peace and balance in your life.

References

- Harris, D. (2014). *10% Happier: How I Tamed the Voice in My Head, Reduced Stress Without Losing My Edge, and Found Self-Help That Actually Works*. HarperCollins.
- Neff, K. D. (2011). *Self-Compassion: The Proven Power of Being Kind to Yourself*. William Morrow.
- American Psychological Association. (2020). *Stress in America™ 2020: A National Mental Health Crisis*. https://www.apa.org/news/press/releases/stress/2020/report-october
- Covey, S. R. (1989). *The 7 Habits of Highly Effective People: Powerful Lessons in Personal Change*. Simon & Schuster.
- Kabat-Zinn, J. (1994). *Wherever You Go, There You Are: Mindfulness Meditation in Everyday Life*. Hyperion.

- Seligman, M. E. P. (2002). *Authentic Happiness: Using the New Positive Psychology to Realize Your Potential for Lasting Fulfillment*. Free Press.

****

Chapter 13

7 Steps You can Take Right Now In The Face of Overwhelming Anxiety

Step 1: Recognize and Acknowledge Your Anxiety

The first step in dealing with overwhelming anxiety is to recognize and acknowledge its presence. Denying or suppressing your feelings can lead to increased stress and anxiety. Instead, take a moment to notice your anxiety without judgment. Acknowledge that it is a natural response to stress or uncertainty, and that it is okay to feel this way.

Step 2: Practice Deep Breathing

Deep breathing is a powerful tool for calming the mind and body. When you're feeling anxious, take a few minutes to focus on your breath. Inhale slowly through your nose, filling your lungs completely, and then exhale slowly through your mouth. Repeat this process for several minutes until you feel a sense of calm. Deep breathing can help activate the body's relaxation response, reducing anxiety and promoting relaxation.

Step 3: Ground Yourself in the Present Moment

Anxiety often arises from worries about the future or ruminations about the past. To combat this, ground yourself in the present moment through mindfulness. Pay attention to your surroundings, the sensations in your body, and the sounds you hear. Focusing on the here and now can help break the cycle of anxious thoughts and bring you back to a state of calm.

Step 4: Use Positive Affirmations

Positive affirmations can help counteract negative thoughts and self-talk that contribute to anxiety. Choose affirmations that resonate with you, such as "I am calm and in control" or "I am capable of handling whatever comes my way." Repeat these affirmations to yourself, especially during moments of anxiety, to remind yourself of your strength and resilience.

Step 5: Engage in Physical Activity

Physical activity is an effective way to reduce anxiety. Exercise releases endorphins, which are natural mood lifters, and helps distract you from anxious thoughts. Whether it's a brisk walk, yoga, or a workout at the gym, find an activity that you enjoy and make it a part of your routine. Regular exercise can help reduce overall levels of anxiety and improve your sense of well-being.

Step 6: Connect with Others

Social support is crucial when dealing with anxiety. Reach out to friends, family, or a support group to share your feelings and experiences. Talking to others can provide a sense of perspective, validation, and connection. Knowing that you are not alone in your struggles can be a great source of comfort and strength.

Step 7: Seek Professional Help

If your anxiety feels overwhelming or persistent, it may be time to seek professional help. A mental health professional, such as a therapist or counselor, can provide you with tools and strategies to manage your anxiety effectively. They can also help you explore the underlying causes of your anxiety and develop a personalized plan for coping with it.

Each of these steps offers a way to navigate anxiety with grace and inner peace. By incorporating these practices into your life, you can build resilience and find calm in the midst of life's storms.

****

Chapter 14

7 Steps You Can Take Right Now To Help You With Difficulty in Managing Negative Thoughts and Toxic Self-talk

Step 1: Recognize and Label Negative Thoughts

The first step in managing negative thoughts and toxic self-talk is to recognize them as they occur. Pay attention to your internal dialogue and notice when negative thoughts arise. Label them as just thoughts, not facts. For example, if you think, "I'm not good enough," label it as a "negative thought" instead of accepting it as truth. This creates a separation between you and the thought, making it easier to challenge and manage.

Step 2: Challenge Negative Thoughts

Once you've recognized and labeled a negative thought, challenge its validity. Ask yourself questions like, "Is this thought based on facts or assumptions?" and "What evidence do I have to support or refute this thought?" By questioning the accuracy of your negative thoughts, you can begin to see them as distortions rather than truths, reducing their power over you.

Step 3: Reframe Negative Thoughts

Reframing involves changing the way you interpret a situation or thought. Instead of accepting a negative thought as it is, try to reframe it in a more positive or neutral light. For example, if you think, "I always fail," reframe it to, "I've faced challenges before, but I've also had successes." This helps shift your perspective and fosters a more balanced and constructive mindset.

Step 4: Practice Mindfulness

Mindfulness is the practice of being present and fully engaged in the moment without judgment. By practicing mindfulness, you can observe your thoughts without getting caught up in them. Techniques like meditation, deep breathing, and body scans can help you develop mindfulness and increase your awareness of your thought patterns.

Step 5: Use Positive Affirmations

Positive affirmations are statements that you repeat to yourself to counteract negative thoughts and reinforce positive beliefs. Choose affirmations that resonate with you and address the specific negative thoughts you're struggling with. For example, if you often think, "I'm not capable," use an affirmation like, "I am capable and strong." Repeat these affirmations regularly to help reprogram your thought patterns.

Step 6: Cultivate Self-Compassion

Self-compassion involves treating yourself with kindness, understanding, and forgiveness. It's about recognizing that everyone makes mistakes and experiences challenges. When you notice negative thoughts or self-talk, respond with compassion rather than criticism. Remind yourself that it's okay to be imperfect and that you're doing your best.

Step 7: Seek Support

Managing negative thoughts and toxic self-talk can be challenging, and it's okay to seek support. Talk to friends, family, or a mental health professional about your experiences. Sharing your struggles with someone you trust can provide validation, perspective, and encouragement. You don't have to navigate this journey alone.

By implementing these steps, you can develop strategies to manage negative thoughts and toxic self-talk, leading to greater inner peace and resilience. Remember, this is a process, and it's okay to take it one step at a time.

****

Chapter 15

7 Steps You can Take Right Now To Help You Maintain Peace and Calm In Turbulent Times

Step 1: Prioritize Self-Care

In turbulent times, self-care becomes essential for maintaining peace and calm. Prioritize activities that nurture your physical, emotional, and mental well-being, such as getting enough sleep, eating nutritious foods, exercising regularly, and engaging in hobbies or activities that bring you joy. Self-care acts as a foundation for resilience, enabling you to better cope with stress and challenges.

Step 2: Establish a Routine

Creating a routine can provide a sense of stability and normalcy in the midst of chaos. Establish a daily schedule that includes time for work, rest, self-care, and activities that help you relax and unwind. Consistency in your routine can help reduce anxiety and create a sense of predictability and control.

Step 3: Practice Mindfulness and Meditation

Mindfulness and meditation are powerful tools for cultivating inner peace. Set aside time each day to practice mindfulness or meditation, focusing on the present moment and letting go of worries about the past or future. These practices can help you stay centered and calm, even in the face of uncertainty.

Step 4: Limit Exposure to Negative News and Social Media

Excessive exposure to negative news and social media can amplify anxiety and stress. Be mindful of your media consumption and set boundaries to protect your mental health. Choose to engage with content that uplifts and inspires you, rather than content that fuels fear and negativity.

Step 5: Cultivate Gratitude

Gratitude has the power to shift your focus from what's wrong to what's right in your life. Make a habit of acknowledging and appreciating the good things, no matter how small. Keeping a gratitude journal or sharing what you're thankful for with loved ones can enhance your sense of well-being and help you maintain a positive outlook.

Step 6: Connect with Others

Maintaining social connections is crucial for emotional support and resilience. Reach out to friends, family, or support groups to share your feelings and experiences. Lean on your community for comfort and encouragement, and offer the same in return. Remember, you're not alone in navigating life's challenges.

Step 7: Seek Professional Help if Needed

If you're struggling to manage negative thoughts and maintain peace and calm, don't hesitate to seek professional help. A therapist or counselor can provide you with coping strategies, support, and guidance tailored to your specific needs. Investing in your mental health is a sign of strength, not weakness.

By implementing these steps, you can create a personal toolkit for navigating turbulent times with grace and inner peace. Remember that it's okay to take things one day at a time and to be gentle with yourself as you navigate life's storms.

****

Chapter 16

7 Steps You Can Take Right Now To Find Balance and Harmony Amidst Chaos

Step 1: Identify Your Priorities

Finding balance and harmony amidst chaos begins with identifying your priorities. Take some time to reflect on what is truly important to you in your personal and professional life. Determine which aspects of your life need more attention and which areas you can scale back on. By aligning your actions with your priorities, you can create a more balanced and fulfilling life.

Step 2: Set Boundaries

Setting boundaries is crucial for maintaining balance and harmony. Clearly define your limits with work, relationships, and personal time. Learn to say no to demands that exceed your capacity or conflict with your priorities. Setting boundaries helps you protect your time and energy, allowing you to focus on what matters most.

Step 3: Practice Mindfulness

Mindfulness is the practice of being fully present and engaged in the moment. Incorporate mindfulness techniques into your daily routine, such as deep breathing, meditation, or mindful walking. By staying present, you can reduce stress and anxiety, and cultivate a sense of inner peace even in the midst of chaos.

Step 4: Cultivate Gratitude

Gratitude has the power to shift your focus from what is lacking to what is abundant in your life. Make a habit of acknowledging and appreciating the good things, no matter how small. Keeping a gratitude journal or expressing thanks to others can enhance your sense of well-being and help you maintain a positive outlook.

Step 5: Seek Support

Finding balance and harmony is not a solitary journey. Seek support from friends, family, or a professional therapist when needed. Sharing your experiences and challenges with others can provide you with different perspectives, emotional support, and practical advice to navigate life's chaos.

Step 6: Prioritize Self-Care

Self-care is essential for maintaining balance and harmony. Prioritize activities that nourish your body, mind, and soul, such as exercise, healthy eating, rest, and hobbies that bring you joy. By taking care of yourself, you can enhance your resilience and ability to cope with stress.

Step 7: Embrace Flexibility

Flexibility is key to finding balance and harmony amidst chaos. Recognize that life is unpredictable and that it's okay to adjust your plans and expectations as circumstances change. Embracing flexibility allows you to navigate challenges with grace and adapt to the ebb and flow of life.

By implementing these steps, you can create a personal roadmap for finding balance and harmony amidst chaos. Remember that balance is not a static state but an ongoing process of adjustment and alignment with your values and priorities.

****

Chapter 17

7 Steps You Can Take Right Now To Create Practical Strategies To Cope With Life's Pressures

Step 1: Identify Your Stressors

The first step in creating practical strategies to cope with life's pressures is to identify your stressors. Take note of the situations, people, or tasks that consistently trigger stress or anxiety. Understanding what causes your stress is essential for developing targeted coping strategies.

Step 2: Develop a Stress Management Plan

Once you've identified your stressors, develop a stress management plan. This plan should include specific actions you can take to address each stressor. For example, if tight deadlines at work are a source of stress, your plan might include breaking down projects into smaller tasks and setting achievable deadlines for each.

Step 3: Practice Relaxation Techniques

Incorporate relaxation techniques into your daily routine to help manage stress. Techniques such as deep breathing, progressive muscle relaxation, meditation, or yoga can activate your body's relaxation response, reducing stress and promoting a sense of calm.

Step 4: Establish Healthy Boundaries

Setting healthy boundaries is crucial for managing life's pressures. Clearly communicate your limits to others, and learn to say no to requests or commitments that exceed your capacity. Protecting your time and energy is essential for maintaining your well-being.

Step 5: Prioritize Self-Care

Make self-care a priority. Engage in activities that nourish your body, mind, and spirit, such as exercise, healthy eating, getting enough sleep, and pursuing hobbies or interests that bring you joy. Regular self-care can enhance your resilience and ability to cope with stress.

Step 6: Seek Social Support

Build a strong support network of friends, family, or colleagues who can provide emotional support and practical assistance when needed. Sharing your challenges and seeking advice from others can help you feel less isolated and more equipped to handle life's pressures.

Step 7: Practice Mindful Acceptance

Learn to practice mindful acceptance of situations you cannot change. Recognize that some aspects of life are beyond your control, and focus your energy on what you can influence. Accepting what you cannot change can help reduce feelings of frustration and anxiety.

By following these steps, you can create practical strategies to cope with life's pressures, helping you navigate challenges with grace and inner peace. Remember, coping with stress is an ongoing process, and it's important to be flexible and adapt your strategies as needed.

****

Epilogue:

The Journey Continues

As we close the pages of "Unleash Your Calm: Navigating Life's Storms with Grace and Inner Peace," it's important to remember that the journey to inner peace is ongoing. The strategies and insights shared in this book are not one-time solutions but rather tools to be used and refined throughout your life. Embracing the principles of mindfulness, self-awareness, gratitude, and resilience will empower you to face life's challenges with grace and maintain a sense of calm amidst the chaos.

Reflecting on Your Progress

Take a moment to reflect on the progress you've made since embarking on this journey. Celebrate the moments of calm you've experienced, the negative thoughts you've transformed, and the balance you've cultivated in your life. Acknowledge the challenges you've faced and the resilience you've demonstrated in overcoming them.

Embracing the Ongoing Journey

The path to inner peace is not linear. There will be times when you feel in harmony with yourself and the world, and times when you feel off balance. This is normal and expected. What matters is your commitment to continuing the journey, using the tools and strategies you've learned to navigate the storms that come your way.

Staying Connected to Your Inner Calm

As you move forward, remember to stay connected to your inner calm. Make mindfulness and meditation a regular part of your routine, practice gratitude daily, and continue to challenge and reframe negative thoughts. Seek support from others when needed, and don't hesitate to revisit the chapters of this book for guidance and inspiration.

Sharing Your Journey

Consider sharing your journey with others. Your experiences and insights can be a source of encouragement and support for those also seeking inner peace. Whether through conversations with friends, participation in support groups, or sharing your story online, your journey can inspire others to embark on their own path to inner peace.

Final Thoughts

The journey to inner peace is one of the most rewarding journeys you can undertake. It requires courage, commitment, and compassion, but the rewards are immeasurable. As you continue to navigate life's storms with grace, remember that you have the tools and strength to unleash your calm and cultivate a life of balance, harmony, and inner peace.

May your journey to inner peace be filled with grace, growth, and a deep sense of calm.

****

About This Author

James C. Tanner is a highly published writer, who has written and published for over 38 years.

Starting as a song writer, his first collection of over 200 lyric sets were published at age 16.

He has written and taught under contract, business skills development programs for clients such as, The Government of Canada.

He is a former professional Investigator who specialized in cult/occult related matters, with a targeted focus on the ritual slaughter of animals.

With a writing portfolio which includes many genres, James C. Tanner has written heavily in areas of business, marketing, psychology, personal motivation and human interest.

Over the course of years, James C. Tanner has published almost exclusively under pen names utilizing 5 different pen names, each assigned to specific writing genres. In recent years, he has begun to publish under his own name.

In June of 2007, when tallies were gathered from all publishers, it was discovered that James C. Tanner's monthly writings were reaching an average monthly audience of over 12 million readers.

Today, James C. Tanner lives the quiet life of a writer tucked away in the vineyard country of Kelowna, British Columbia, Canada.

****

Other Books By This Author

Ancient Healthy Recipes for Modern Plates:

The Real Mediterranean Diet Unveiled

Know When To Pivot:

Navigating Uncertainty With Confidence

Rise Above:

Breaking Chains to Overcome Unhealthy Habits

Embracing a More Fulfilling Life

Gluten Free Mexican Recipes:

Enjoying The Flavours of Ol' Mexico

Rising from the Ashes:

Reclaiming Your Life after Narcissistic Abuse

Beyond The Agony Of Chronic Pain:

Finding Relief and Understanding

Release Your Greatness:

Breaking Free To Live A Purposeful...Limitless Life

Rest Now My Love:

Coping With The Loss Of A Life Partner

Failing Forward – Rising Stronger!

Rekindling Hope In A Crazy World

Daring To Dream A Bigger...Better Dream

Why He Doesn't Love You Anymore

Reshaping Your World – When Relationships Require Necessary Endings

The Emotions Mastery Handbook:

Mastering Your Emotional Intelligence for a Life of Fulfillment

Wild Savory Adventures:

Mastering the Art of Cooking Wild Game

AI Prompt Power:

Unleashing AI To Create Passive Income

From Lot To Loot:

A Comprehensive Guide to "No-Money-Down" Land Flipping Deals in America

Excelling In The Face of Personal Chaos

A Very Plain Amish Christmas Cookbook

****